When
Good People
Quarrel

When Good People Quarrel

Studies of Conflict Resolution

Robert S. Kreider and
Rachel Waltner Goossen

Foreword by Ron Kraybill

HERALD PRESS
Scottdale, Pennsylvania
Kitchener, Ontario.

Library of Congress Cataloging-in-Publication Data

Kreider, Robert S.
  When good people quarrel : studies of conflict resolution /
Robert S. Kreider and Rachel Waltner Goossen : foreword by Ron
Kraybill.
        p. cm.
     Bibliography: p.
     Includes index.
     ISBN 0-8361-3469-9
        1. Interpersonal conflict—United States—Case studies.
2. Conflict management—United States—Case studies. 3. Conflict
management—Religious aspects—Christianity—Case studies.
4. Church controversies—Case studies. 5. Community and school—
United States—Case studies. I. Goossen, Rachel Waltner.
II. Title.
HM132.K69   1989
302.3'4—dc19   88-35688
                                                                      CIP

The paper used in this publication meets the minimum requirements of
American National Standard for Information Sciences—Permanence of
Paper for Printed Library Materials, ANSI Z39.48-1984.

For Scripture permissions, see page 10.

WHEN GOOD PEOPLE QUARREL
Copyright © 1989 by Herald Press, Scottdale, Pa. 15683
     Published simultaneously in Canada by Herald Press,
     Kitchener, Ont. N2G 4M5. All rights reserved.
Library of Congress Catalog Card Number: 88-35688
International Standard Book Number: 0-8361-3469-9
Printed in the United States of America
Design by Jim Butti

95 94 93 92 91 90 89 10 9 8 7 6 5 4 3 2 1

CONTENTS

ACKNOWLEDGMENTS

We are indebted to a number of former students who wrote papers or contributed services: Ken Bachman, Barry Bartel, Mark Becker, Karen Enns, David Kreider, David Lohrentz, Joseph Miller, Rachel Moyer, and others. Ron Kraybill contributed the original draft for case study Number 13. Herman F. Ressig is the author of Number 17, a short drama inspired by Isaiah 2:4 that first appeared in *Christianity and Crisis*, May 11, 1959. We are also grateful to many people who shared their stories orally.

Some of the analytical models contained in this volume appeared first in Adam Curle, *Making Peace* (1971); David Augsburger, *Caring Enough to Confront* (1980); Richard E. Walton, *Interpersonal Peacemaking*, 1969; and Roger Fisher and William Ury, *Getting to Yes* (1981). We are grateful for permission to reproduce these materials.

We appreciate the counsel of Ron Kraybill, John Paul Lederach, and David Brubaker of the Mennonite Conciliation Service. David Brubaker prepared questions for most of the case studies. All three helped to select analytical models for the section "Guidelines and Models for Understanding Conflicts."

Rachel Waltner Goossen and Robert Kreider

PERMISSIONS FOR SCRIPTURE QUOTATION

FOREWORD

This book is significant because it begins with the assumption that conflict is a part of life; it opens the closet door on conflict. With dignity, it recounts intense disagreements between good folks like you and me. I hear this as an invitation—one good story, simply and honestly told, invites another. People who gather to hear these stories will find their own stories pressing forward in memory, aching to be told and heard.

Everyone experiences conflict. Wherever people are alive and growing, they rub shoulders in ways that chafe. As a gray-haired farmer once said, "The only place there's no conflict is in the graveyard." Thus skill in conflict is pivotal for anyone committed to personal growth.

The problem is that no one seems to believe this. People study a wide range of topics, but they rarely study how to be skillful in conflict. Churches and organizations plan and prepare for many things, but they don't prepare for disagreements. Young people hear about the joys of love and marriage; rarely do they hear about the pain of inevitable conflict. In many ways, our society pretends that conflict does not exist.

The starting point for effectiveness in conflict is accepting that it is normal, that good people do disagree. A friend recently reflected on a stressful situation in her congregation. "It made a big difference," she commented, "just remembering that it's okay to have conflict. I kept reminding myself that these moments are a normal part of healthy church life. Each time I remembered that I felt calmer and more able to hear others."

People who try hardest to avoid conflict often end up with the gravest injuries. Such a paradox! In conflict resolution seminars, I tell people, "If you want to have less conflict, invite disagreement!" Inviting disagreement offers choice.

In a congregational business meeting a member rises to state an emotionally charged opinion. The moderator must respond. Rather than freezing in fear and chiding the speaker for being uncharitable, the moderator thanks the speaker for a clear statement and invites other viewpoints as well. By welcoming expressions of diversity the moderator helps everyone stay calm and thoughtful.

Two colleagues are arguing. They resist the temptation to say, in tone if not in words, "I am absolutely right and don't you dare disagree with me!" Instead, they welcome differing views. "This is the way I see things, but I might be missing something and I'd really like to hear how you see it differently."

A husband and wife are traveling home from a party. He senses that she is critical of his social habits. But he does not withdraw, thereby establishing that disagreement on this issue is intolerable. Rather, he invites her comments. "I'm doing the best I can in social settings and I think I'm doing pretty well. But I'm willing to hear ideas on how I might do better."

This volume holds great promise for readers as well as grave responsibility. There is promise here because storytelling is the beginning of hope. Christians know that confession is the first step to release from sin. Describing that which has bound us is a major step toward freedom. To invite storytelling, as this book does, is to invite healing.

This brings with it serious responsibility. Wherever stories are told, there must be careful listening. An open, attentive listener nurtures healing; a listener who is quick to judge or advise blocks healing.

Sometimes a story calls for more than listening. Behind every account in the book looms the question: How can one be a minister of reconciliation to those wounded by conflict? Discussion groups must be prepared to confront the same question in their own experiences.

Healing in the end must take us beyond our own stories. We need new ways of thinking about ourselves and new skills for communicating with others. Here the book provides simple analytical models, questions to focus discussion, and bibliographic resources.

Perhaps most importantly, this volume places before us selections from what Christians hold as the Original Story. Rarely have we viewed the Bible as a study in conflict resolution. Yet the struggle for reconciliation amid brokenness recurs in virtually every chapter. Reconciliation is the center of God's purpose. Thus the promise of ultimate healing springs from encounter with the Original Story.

No one in Scripture—not even Jesus—represents a consistent model for conflict resolution. What matters in the Original Story is not technical perfection, but commitment to extend oneself in order to reconcile. For this reason, Christians claim Jesus as Lord. For this reason also, the volume calls us to participate in the Original Story. We belong here, not because we are already healed. Rather, we belong because we have committed ourselves, in the name of the Prince of Peace, to being ministers of reconciliation.

Ron Kraybill
Mennonite Conciliation Service
December 1988

AUTHORS' PREFACE

A young high school coach is fired after two losing seasons. His wife, who has heard the angry taunts of fans at the games, feels that she failed to give her husband adequate support.

A congregation is split evenly over the issue of whether to build a new educational wing or to remodel the existing facilities so that they can be used more hours of the week.

A group of businesspersons in a town near a large city, eager to attract industry, urge that a public meeting be held to consider lifting the ban on liquor sales in local restaurants.

A once gifted but now faltering organist clings to her organ position to the exasperation of the congregation, but no one wants to speak out for fear of offending the elderly woman or her extended family.

A farm couple loses the family farm through foreclosure. The despondent husband leaves the community; the wife, who finds a job, reports that no one in her congregation has talked to her about the double tragedy in her life.

These are the kinds of conflicts that occur in every community. Here we offer twenty-five mostly ordinary conflicts for study and discussion, designed to heighten awareness of the conflict and resolution processes that accompany the human experience. These case studies or stories are derived from ten years of classroom teaching of conflict resolution. Some in the collection were generated by students in oral and written presentations.

This sourcebook has been prepared for several audiences: church members, students, and general readers. Christians are called to be ministers of reconciliation; a major arena where reconciliation may occur is the congregation. Church members often need help in understanding the nature of conflict and in developing the skills of peacemaking. The stories that follow reveal that peacemaking is expressed by persons in varied roles: the activist, advocate, mediator, researcher. While church members are intended as the primary reading audience, this collection also includes stories useful for courses in ethics, social work, and peace studies. Finally, it is designed as a resource for those who are interested in developing competency in conflict resolution.

These stories are close to the experiences of readers. The conflicts take place among family and friends and within congregation, school, and community. Some of the disputes are drawn from the experiences of a historic peace church people, the Mennonites. A people long opposed to war must grapple continuously with conflicts that arise in their own lives. Such stories, out of a particular body of experience, inescapably touch universal issues.

The studies have been edited to permit ample time for groups to discuss and, in some instances, to role play. Guidelines for role playing appear in the appendix. Questions designed to stimulate group discussion appear at the end of each case study. A few of the accounts are longer and provide fuller description of complex conflicts. Resourceful readers and discussion leaders will use a variety of methods to help participants see the conflict as ones that could occur in their own congregations or communities. Groups discussing conflicts may wish to invite persons experienced in counseling and mediation to join them for the examination of particular cases.

These studies are based on one or more actual experiences. In most, however, fictional names and details are used to protect sources. In all cases where actual names have been used, the story has appeared in the public record or it has the approval of persons involved.

We hope that readers will supplement the resources of this collection by gathering information and writing about conflicts and their resolutions from experiences close at hand. In describing a conflict the writer should set the events in context and seek to reflect accurately the divergent points of view. The writer should invite several parties to read the draft for completeness and fairness to all involved.

Distributed throughout this volume is a second set of "case studies" of conflict resolution, excerpted from the Bible. The inclusion of these scriptural stories, with accompanying questions, affirms that throughout Old and New Testament times people grappled with conflicts, sometimes redemptively, sometimes injuriously. Thus the Bible is, among many things, a study of conflict resolution. In the section "Guidelines and Models for Understanding Conflicts" are several simple analytical models for understanding and responding to conflicts. These models point to a growing body of literature on conflict resolution theory.

The parallel presentation of case studies from current experience and from the Bible, plus accompanying analytical models, suggests the interplay between theory and practice, professional and amateur. We hope that these varied resources will alert the reader to the ever-present occurrence of conflicts among us. Second, we hope these resources will remind us that where there is conflict we are called to be peacemakers.

The conflicts presented in this volume are micro conflicts, that is, conflicts of relatively small scale. These micro conflicts are not unlike the macro conflicts of national and international proportions. The biblical writer James reminds us:

> What causes conflicts and quarrels among you? Do they not spring from the aggressiveness of your bodily desires? You want something which you cannot have, and so you are bent on murder; you are envious, and cannot attain your ambition, and so you quarrel and fight. You do not get what you want, because you do not pray for it. Or, if you do, your requests are not granted because you pray from wrong motives, to spend what you get on your pleasures. (James 4:1-3)

This volume invites the reader to find ways of resolving the little wars among and around us.

Rachel Waltner Goossen and Robert S. Kreider

When
Good People
Quarrel

Family and Interpersonal

Three Steps in Resolving Conflict

If your brother commits a sin, go and take the matter up with him, strictly between yourselves, and if he listens to you, you have won your brother over. If he will not listen, take one or two others with you, so that all facts may be duly established on the evidence of two or three witnesses. If he refuses to listen to them, report the matter to the congregation; and if he will not listen even to the congregation you must then treat him as you would a pagan or a tax-gatherer.

I tell you this: whatever you forbid on earth shall be forbidden in heaven, and whatever you allow on earth shall be allowed in heaven. (Matthew 18:15-18)

Questions

1. How can this three-step procedure be helpful in resolving conflict?

2. Why is this method not more often used?

3. What kind of church would we have if every Christian followed these steps?

1.
Yielding to Avoid Conflict

The Old Testament describes life among Hebrews just as it was: the ugly with the beautiful, the embarrassing with the pleasant. The Bible includes true stories of quarrels, murder, theft, lying, cheating, and cruelty. The biblical writers did not lock closets which held family or community skeletons. The Old Testament also tells of love and forgiveness, faithfulness and courage, resourcefulness and fairness. Many biblical stories of conflict lead to experiences of reconciliation.

The first case study in each of the three sections of this book is a paraphrase of a conflict recorded in the Bible. Distributed throughout the volume are many stories which could be elaborated and rewritten to serve as present-day case studies of conflict resolution. The following story about land and water rights paraphrases a conflict found in the thirteenth chapter of Genesis.

Abram and his nephew Lot had come as immigrants to a country of fertile plains, mountain valleys, and scattered springs. Abram and Lot, uncle and nephew, worked closely in many farming and ranch enterprises: cattle and sheep buying, sheep shearing, marketing, and water improvement projects. Both had accumulated huge herds of cattle and flocks of sheep. To handle their extensive operations, each employed large staffs of cowhands and shepherds.

As their ranching expanded, problems mounted. The two men overgrazed the best pastures. Too few wells, springs, and ponds were available to meet the needs of the big herds and flocks. The two family groups began to lose the spirit of kinship. Lot's hired men and Abram's hired men jostled for position at the watering places. Tempers flared. Disputes led to blows. Abram and Lot observed outbreaks of hostility between their two family groups. Both found it difficult to cool the hotheads among their workers. Abram went to his nephew and said: "This quarreling is getting out of hand. When you and I came to this country, we were one big caring family. Things have changed and it's not the way you and I would like to live." Lot responded: "The problem, I think, is water. Both of us have taken on new hired hands who think that the only way to speak is with elbows and fists." Abram added, "We tried, you know, to set up some understandings on water use, but we have to admit that this country is getting too crowded for all of us." Lot assented sadly: "Maybe you are right. And yet, maybe we could dig more wells."

Abram was silent for a time and then responded: "We are a peaceful people. We do not want this quarreling between your workers and ours, your family and ours. There are tens of thousands of acres out there. Let us separate and put a little space between us. I heard a wise man once say, 'Good fences make good neighbors.' So, if you go left, I will go right; if you go right, I will go left."

Lot and Abram were standing on a high ridge. Lot looked east and saw the broad, well-watered Jordan Valley which stretched south as far as the eye could see. The soil was deep and fertile. He thought to himself: "I could move into grain farming and could cut back on cattle and sheep. I wouldn't be away from home so much." To the west Lot saw the hill country, range upon range. Some upland valleys had small patches suitable for farming, but most of the rugged hills would be better for grazing.

Lot decided quickly, "I choose the plain to the east."

Abram said, "Fine, we'll take to the hills."

They embraced and wished each other well. Each went his way with his extended family, workers, and herds and flocks.

This decision closed a major chapter in each of their lives. Lot settled near one of the prosperous cities on the plain. Abram, the older man, moved with his people into the hills where they pioneered in harsh country. The old quarrels at the waterholes ended, but soon Lot and Abram encountered new sets of problems.

Questions

1. What steps did Abram and Lot take to resolve the conflict? Did Abram give in too easily?

2. What is the difference between friendly and hostile separation? When is separation appropriate? When is it inappropriate?

Paying Off Your Opponent

Now about that time Abimelech, with Phicol the commander of his army, addressed Abraham in these terms: "God is with you in all that you do. Now swear an oath to me in the name of God, that you will not break faith with me, my offspring, or my descendants. As I have kept faith with you, so shall you keep faith with me and with the country where you have come to live as an alien." Abraham said, "I swear."

It happened that Abraham had a complaint against Abimelech about a well which Abimelech's men had seized. Abimelech said, "I do not know who did this. You never told me, and I have heard nothing about it till now." So Abraham took sheep and cattle and gave them to Abimelech; and the two of them made a pact. Abraham set seven ewe-lambs apart, and when Abimelech asked him why he had set these lambs apart he said, "Accept these from me in token that I dug this well." Therefore that place was called Beersheba, because there the two of them swore an oath. When they had made the pact at Beersheba, Abimelech and Phicol the commander of his army returned at once to the country of the Philistines, and Abraham planted a strip of ground at Beersheba. (Genesis 21:22-33)

Questions
1. Did Abimelech owe payment to Abraham for the stolen well?
2. Was Abraham opening himself to more attacks?

2.
Family Tension over Inheritance

Money liberates people from poverty, undergirds good causes, and is the lifeblood of the economy. Love of money also corrupts, is "the root of all evil" (1 Timothy 6:10), and can divide families and congregations. One person's concern for justice can be seen by another as a spirit of covetousness. Each of the following six stories offers a different perspective on the quest for justice and unity among imperfect members of a family.

a. The Terrible-Tempered Younger Brother

Grandfather had an ability to make money. He acquired farms, town rental properties, and about half interest in a small food-processing plant. He had five sons and one daughter by his first wife and one son by his second wife. Five sons and a son-in-law were farmers. But the youngest son, the only son of the second wife, lived in town, worked in the family business, and married the daughter of a partner in the business.

The five older sons were quiet, unassertive men. The youngest son, a half-brother to the five, was much more assertive and talkative. He had been in the army for a few months in World War I and was an active member of the American Legion. At family gatherings he told stories of famous persons and athletes he had met during his travels. His brothers listened attentively and with apparent appreciation. The youngest son had a fiery temper and often exploded when he was at the factory, particularly when he did not get his way.

In my grandfather's will the company stock was divided equally among his six sons and one daughter. The sons attending board meetings as stockholders did not enjoy the meetings because of their youngest brother's frequent flare-ups. They explained their brother's behavior as the result of the protective indulgence of their stepmother for her only son. He was a good promoter and salesman; the business succeeded.

Many years after his father's death, the youngest brother asked to buy his five brothers' and his sister's stock in the company. He offered to pay approximately what the value of the stock had been years earlier when the estate had been settled. The brothers and sister agreed. They wanted to distance themselves from uncomfortable personal relations in the factory, and they did not raise questions with their brother regarding the fairness of the sale price.

Several years later the brother, having acquired majority control of the company, sold the company to a larger firm at ten times the value per share he had paid earlier. The brothers did not protest that their youngest brother had taken advantage of them, but several wives were critical of him. Two grandchildren felt that, had their parents received their just worth of the estate, two of the original farms could have been kept in the family. One granddaughter commented, "The money isn't important. I just wish the brothers had stood up to their youngest brother and told him that he was cheating them out of their inheritance. But all their lives they walked away from unpleasant dealings with their spoiled, terrible-tempered younger brother."

Getting Rid of Your Rival

Abel was a shepherd and Cain a tiller of the soil. The day came when Cain brought some of the produce of the soil as a gift to the Lord; and Abel brought some of the first-born of his flock, the fat portions of them. The Lord received Abel and his gift with favour; but Cain and his gift he did not receive. Cain was very angry and his face fell. Then the Lord said to Cain, "Why are you so angry and cast down? If you do well, you are accepted, if not, sin is a demon crouching at the door. It shall be eager for you, and you will be mastered by it."

Cain said to his brother Abel, "Let us go into the open country." While they were there, Cain attacked his brother Abel and murdered him. Then the Lord said to Cain, "Where is your brother Abel?" Cain answered, "I do not know. Am I my brother's keeper?" (Genesis 4:3-9)

Question
Other than murder, what methods do people use to rid themselves of their rivals?

b. *Another Side to the Story*

Grandfather owned the town's largest business. He had a daughter who moved to a distant state. Two sons were with him in the business. The younger son, a widower with four small children, remarried and died a few years later. Grandfather's estate was divided into three equal parts—one third of the stock of the business to a daughter, one third to the older son, and one third to the three children of the younger, deceased son. The older son continued to manage the business, which prospered. He also served as guardian and financial manager for the four children.

The four children married, had families, lived in different communities and became well established financially. Their uncle offered to buy their shares of stock in the family business so that they could purchase homes or invest in businesses. The amount offered seemed to each like a great deal of money. They agreed to the sale.

About ten years later, the uncle sold all the shares in the company for a price many times higher than he had paid to the four children. He had devoted forty years of his life to the company. Although he had received a good salary, he felt he was entitled to the increased value represented by the sale of the stock. The four children felt that their uncle had taken advantage of them in the stock purchase but they did not confront him. When their uncle was lauded for his benevolence, they would say to each other, "But there is another side to the story."

c. *A Clash Between a Father and His Children*

A widower in his seventies owned a section of good Nebraska farmland. He had three daughters and one son, all married. A family employed in town rented the home-place. The retired farmer lived in town. His son, who owned land and had a large farming operation, rented all of his father's 640 acres.

The father had stated to representatives of his church college and conference that he wanted to give one quarter of his estate to the college and one quarter to the conference. He had discussed this with his wife, who agreed with the plan.

When the father told the children of his decision, they voiced in various ways their objections. All four had received financial help from their parents for their educations and for buying homes. All were well established and had no special financial needs. However, some were fearful that gifts to the college and conference would force a breakup of the family farm. The son said he couldn't afford to buy the half-section the father was proposing to give to the college and the conference. Some were not enthusiastic about the two causes he and his wife had selected.

The father, who wanted the full support of his children, informed the college and the conference that he would need to postpone his decision on the gifts. He was troubled and asked a good friend for counsel.

d. *Asking the Pastor to Bring Peace to the Family*

Jacob and Mary Miller were an Oklahoma farm couple in their sixties who farmed 480 acres of land. They had six children, some who lived in the community and some who lived at a distance. After the death of his wife, Jacob made out his will and assigned a particular eighty-acre tract to each one of his six children. Meanwhile, irrigation technology came to the region. Some of the land could be easily irrigated and was highly productive; some of the land was unsuitable for irrigation and, hence, had less value.

Following the introduction of irrigation, Jacob Miller talked occasionally of the need to revise his will, but never took steps to do so. In his last years he became senile and was incapable of revising the will. Following the father's death, the six children learned the details of the will. Each had received a particular eighty-acre plot. The children were informed that some of the eighty-acre plots—the flat, fertile, well-drained land—was worth $1,000 an acre. Some of the hilly land, less suitable for cultivation and irrigation, was worth no more than $300 an acre.

Several children who had received less valuable plots were distressed. They requested that those who had been assigned the more valuable land pay them to help even up the inheritance. Those who had received the $1,000-an-acre land replied that their father knew what he was doing and didn't intend to change the inheritance to units of absolutely equal value. Two sons who received some of the more valuable land had been farm partners with their father and stated that this was their father's way of paying them for their years of helping build up the value of the farm. To this the recipients of $300-an-acre land replied that developments in irrigation had entered the picture since their father had made out his will and that he would have made adjustments in his will had he not been ill.

The family held several meetings to discuss their disagreement. The meetings became heated. Some children refused to attend. Harsh words were exchanged and several of the brothers and sisters stopped talking to each other. Since many of the children were members of the same church, several of them asked the pastor whether he would help bring peace to the family.

Running Away from Your Opponent

Esau bore a grudge against Jacob because of the blessing which his father had given him, and he said to himself, "The time of mourning for my father will soon be here; then I will kill my brother Jacob." When Rebecca was told what her elder son Esau was saying, she called her younger son Jacob, and she said to him, "Esau your brother is threatening to kill you. Now, my son, listen to me. Slip away at once to my brother Laban in Harran. Stay with him for a while until your brother's anger cools. When it has subsided and he forgets what you have done to him, I will send and fetch you back. Why should I lose you both in one day?" (Genesis 27:41-45)

Questions

1. Was Jacob a coward to flee?
2. When may flight be the wiser, even more courageous response?

e. Offers Reached One Million Dollars

John and Sara Yoder operated an eighty-acre dairy farm on the edge of Harrisburg, Pennsylvania. Their farm had excellent buildings and was well kept. The Yoders had four children. The youngest son was the only one who remained in farming and in time he took over the operation of the home farm. The parents prepared a will which gave the youngest son the right after the parents' death to purchase the farm at a set price of $50,000. The income from the sale would be distributed equally among the four children.

Some years after the preparation of the will, the parents died. Meanwhile, the city had expanded and encircled the farm. Land developers competed with each other to give a higher price for such choice land, soon to be incorporated into the city. The offers reached one million dollars for the eighty-acre farm.

The youngest son would receive a huge windfall if he paid $50,000 to the estate and then sold it to developers for one million.

He had worked on the farm with his father for ten years and felt that the will reflected his father's recognition that he had helped to keep the dairy in full operation. The three older children did not want to create family tensions over inheritance. Neither they, nor their younger brother, really needed all the income which would come from the sale of the farm to developers. It was unlikely that the younger brother would resist the attractive offers of the developers once he acquired title to the farm.

The three older children met with the younger brother and asked him whether he felt it would be fair to have some leveling of the inheritance benefits. But the younger brother did not want to discuss the issue. The three older children were not ready to take the issue to court, but they did not feel that it was fair for three to receive $12,500 each and one to receive $962,500. They wondered whether there was anything further they could or should do.

From Appeasement to Reconciliation

Jacob spent that night there; and as a present for his brother Esau he chose from the herds he had with him two hundred she-goats, twenty he-goats, two hundred ewes and twenty rams, thirty milch-camels with their young, forty cows and ten young bulls, twenty she-asses and ten he-asses. He put each herd separately into the care of a servant and said to each, "Go on ahead of me, and leave gaps between the herds." Then he gave these instructions to the first: "When my brother Esau meets you and asks you to whom you belong and where you are going and who owns these beasts you are driving, you are to say, 'They belong to your servant Jacob; he sends them as a present to my lord Esau, and he is behind us.'" He gave the same instructions to the second, to the third, and all the drovers, telling them to say the same thing to Esau when they met him. And they were to add, "Your servant Jacob is behind us"; for he thought, "I will appease him with the present that I have sent on ahead, and afterwards, when I come into his presence, he will perhaps receive me kindly." (*Genesis 32:13-20*)

Questions
1. Was Jacob bribing Esau?
2. Can a bribe be an appropriate means of resolving a conflict?

f. *Taking Care of Obligations Before Death*
Elmer and Etta Hess lived on a dairy farm of ninety acres in Virginia. Within half a mile they had a second farm of 150 acres. Two sons lived nearby on two smaller farms. The father and his two sons worked together in a loose partnership in which they had a jointly owned dairy herd and separate hog and broiler operations. The couple and their two sons lived comfortably and simply. They used much of the income to buy quality farm equipment and to keep their farm buildings in the best condition.

The Hesses had three daughters who had received college educations and then married. They had received some assistance from their parents for their education. Each had held a part-time job in order to finish college debt-free. The three daughters had then moved to different communities about four or five hours' driving distance from their parents.

The two sons each took college courses for a year but preferred farming to additional college. The father, in his late fifties, knew that he should update his will. He and his wife considered giving the home place of ninety acres to the two sons because so much of the profits for the past ten years from their joint farm operations had been returned to the farm in improvements and equipment. The father thought that the 150-acre farm, which had about the same value per acre as the smaller farm, would be divided equally among the five children.

The father tested this idea with his three daughters when they were together at Thanksgiving. They did not have much to say. One commented, "Dad, this is your decision. It is up to you and Mother to decide what is best for you and what is fair for the five of us." He knew his daughters well enough to believe that they had unexpressed questions and doubts. Mr. Hess told his wife afterward:

> I think they were disappointed. Maybe we should talk this over with someone who has experience in these matters. The boys have a lot of unpaid equity invested in the home place. The girls have worked on the farm. They know their brothers have put a lot of time and work into the operation. You can tell that they are dragging their feet because they think there is something a little unfair about it. We don't want to let the farm come between them.

The father discussed his problem with a friend from church. The friend, who worked in the local bank, said, "All I can say, Elmer, is this: take care of your obligations to your sons before you die. Don't leave it to your will."

Questions

1. Discuss the family dynamics in each of these cases. For example, in the first case study, how did the five older sons relate to their hotheaded brother?

2. For each case, decribe alternatives for decision-making that might have led to better feelings on all sides.

3. In "Offers Reached One Million Dollars," assume that you are one of the three older children and that your younger brother refused to discuss the land issue with you. What steps would you take to resolve the issue?

4. In "Taking Care of Obligations Before Death," why do you think the daughters were reluctant to express openly their views to their father?

Reconciliation

Jacob raised his eyes and saw Esau coming towards him with four hundred men, so he divided the children between Leah and Rachel and the two slave-girls. He put the slave-girls with their children in front, Leah with her children next, and Rachel with

Joseph last. He then went on ahead of them, bowing low to the ground seven times as he approached his brother. Esau ran to meet him and embraced him; he threw his arms round him and kissed him, and they wept. When Esau looked up and saw the women and children, he said, "Who are these with you?" Jacob replied, "The children whom God has graciously given to your servant." The slave-girls came near, each with her children, and they bowed low. Then Leah with her children came near and bowed low, and afterwards Joseph and Rachel came near and bowed low also. Esau said, "What was all that company of yours that I met?" And he answered, "It was meant to win favour with you, my lord, Esau answered, "I have more than enough. Keep what is yours, my brother." But Jacob said, "On no account: if I have won your favour, then, I pray, accept this gift from me; for, you see, I come into your presence as into that of a god, and you receive me favourably. Accept this gift which I bring you; for God has been gracious to me, and I have all I want." So he urged him, and he accepted it. (Genesis 33:1-11)

Question

What steps did Jacob follow in seeking to resolve the conflict caused by his deceitful theft of Esau's inheritance?

3.
To Sue or Not to Sue

Ours is a society with many disputes: laws multiply, lawyers increase, and court dockets are overloaded. In a conflict the loser is advised, "If you don't like it, go to court." Often there are more amicable and less expensive ways of resolving disputes. The following four experiences invite us to consider alternatives.

a. *The Lawyer's Offer to Sue for Damages*

Phil Parish, a varsity football player, worked for Johnson Lumber Company the year after he graduated from college. He had worked there summers and part time for seven years. He and another worker were assigned the job of restacking half-ton wooden trusses with a forklift.

One day a truss was almost in place when the forklift sagged, allowing the truss to slip off the fork and onto Phil, who was below directing the operation. The heavy truss pinned Phil to the ground. Fellow workers rolled the truss off his back, but he could not move. Someone called the emergency medical service and he was rushed to a nearby hospital for emergency treatment and X-rays. Doctors discovered that his third vertebra had been cracked. X-rays taken a few days later revealed more serious damage to the vertebrae than they had first detected.

Phil was moved to an urban medical center where he received the care of a neurosurgeon. A CAT scan revealed a fracture in the third vertebra all around the spinal cord and many fissures in other vertebrae. Phil was fitted with a back brace and within ten days left the hospital with strict prohibitions as to his bodily movements. He began a carefully planned program of physical therapy.

During his recuperation Phil received 80 percent of his regular wage through workmen's compensation insurance. The lumber company paid his hospital expenses. Although the company president did not visit Phil in the hospital, he told Phil's parents, when he met them on the street, that if the workmen's compensation ran out before Phil could return to work, the company would find funds to cover his needs.

After several months Phil still could not return to work. He missed a summer of work which he had counted on to pay off college debts. The doctors informed Phil that he could not look forward to heavy labor in the lumberyard, where he had already been identified as a promising candidate for a supervisory position. After seven months Phil was aware that he could not perform many simple physical activities.

Following a complete physical examination eight months after the accident, Phil's doctor explained to him that he would probably have to live with a permanent disability and would need to adjust his vocational plans accordingly. Phil, who had applied for life insurance only a few days before the accident, found that companies were reluctant to write a policy for someone with a disability of undetermined future seriousness. Phil and his wife were faced with a radical life change and uncertainty in their vocational and financial plans.

Phil learned that the lumber company's liability insurance did not provide any hope for a settlement for what appeared to be a permanent disability. The manufacturer of the forklift could not be successfully sued because the firm would argue that the equipment was old and should have been properly maintained or replaced. Fellow workers urged Phil to sue the employer for the permanent disability. A lawyer friend offered to conduct a suit for damages at a reduced fee. Phil was reluctant to sue the company officials because they had been his friends for many years. He did not know how much longer he would be covered by workmen's compensation. But he needed to decide soon whether or not to accept the lawyer's offer to sue for damages.

b. *A Possible Malpractice Suit*

A young woman had surgery for the removal of a cancerous breast. A terrible mistake was made. The healthy breast was removed, necessitating the removal of the other breast. The medical staff responsible had difficulty explaining the grievous error. They were aware of the possibility that the patient might sue for malpractice. She and her family were devout Christians. The hospital was church-sponsored and the doctors were members of her church.

Following the surgery and during her recovery, two nurses attended the woman's needs. Doctors always came in pairs to examine and consult with her. She was aware that they were taking precautions in the event that a malpractice suit might be filed. She and her family, members of a church that opposed suing in court, pondered whether they should file a suit.

Why Not Suffer Injury?

If one of your number has a dispute with another, has he the face to take it to pagan law-courts instead of to the community of God's people? It is God's people who are to judge the world; surely you know that. And if the world is to come before you for judgment, are you incompetent to deal with these trifling cases? Are you not aware that we are to judge angels? How much more, mere matters of business? If therefore you have such business disputes, how can you entrust jurisdiction to outsiders, men who count for nothing in our community? I write this to shame you. Can it be that there is not a single wise man among you able to give a decision in a brother-Christian's cause? Must brother go to law with brother—and before unbelievers? Indeed, you already fall below your standard in going to law with one another at all. Why not rather suffer injury? Why not rather let yourself be robbed? (I Corinthians 6:1-7)

Questions
1. Can one justify suing a fellow Christian in court?
2. Should a Christian sue anyone in court?
3. Why is it better to be robbed or injured than to go to court and win?

c. *Seeking a Court Ruling on an Access Road*

A group of six families bought 120 acres of wooded mountain land for summer vacations and as a possible site for building a cabin. The rancher from whom they bought the land assured them that the road up the mountain to their property had been a publicly used road for more than fifty years. However, the title of land sale did not include a statement of legal-access right. The road led for three miles from a county highway up the mountain through the properties of several owners.

One of the property owners, who occupied land along one mile of the mountain road, was planning a vacation housing development on his several thousand acres. He had acquired his land a few years before the six families purchased their 120 acres and he operated many enterprises. He told the six families that he was displeased they had bought the land. They learned he had wanted to buy it for less than they had paid.

When the families began to build a cabin on their property, necessitating the trucking of building materials to the construction site, the land developer began to threaten the group. He claimed that they had no legal right to the road and that he could lock the gates to stop their passage. During the travel of building-supply trucks up and down the road, the building crews sometimes failed to lock and unlock the gates properly. The land developer became increasingly angry. Repeated efforts to discuss the issues with him resulted in some oral understandings. However, he never agreed to clarify understandings in writing.

The developer threatened again to close the road. One night he fired shots as one of the trucks passed his cabin. The county sheriff intervened, asking the developer to behave.

After six years of efforts to gain an understanding about a right-of-way along the old mountain road, the six families were advised by neighbors to bring suit for the clarification of the legal right-of-way. Only one of the six families had ever been a party in a court suit. They were reluctant, on biblical principle, to turn to the courts. And yet they foresaw that their tract of mountain land could become inaccessible if they did not receive a court ruling that the three miles of road had been a public-access road for many years.

d. *Who Pays for an Official's Mistake?*

John Jones, a building contractor, lives in a house built on the bank of Cottonwood Creek. Nearby are several other quality houses he has built. One fall Jones received a building permit from the county zoning administrator to build a house on a lot by the creek. Jones had begun construction earlier on the basis of oral approval from the county official. He had invested thirty thousand dollars in the project when he received a second letter from the zoning administrator, asking him to halt construction. The county official, who had been on the job only a month before writing the first letter, acknowledged that he had made a mistake.

The house which Jones was building was in the floodway of a stream which might flood once in a hundred years. The county official had learned recently that the county would lose its eligibility for federal flood insurance and federal disaster aid if Jones's house were built in the floodway. The presence of a new home there would nullify the federal insurance loans and disaster aid for all of the 140 owners of buildings in a nearby area on slightly higher ground.

The lot where Jones built the house was zoned for construc-

tion in 1976—seven years before the county joined the federal
flood insurance program. The seven other houses in the subdiv-
sion on the creek bank were exempt from the federal regulations
because they were completed before the county joined the flood
protection program.

John Jones, who had more than a year's income tied up in
the house, was in a quandary. The county commissioners agreed
to ask the federal authorities to exempt the house under construction from the federal regulations but they had little hope of success. The county commissioners could order a deeper dredging of
the creek bed. That would cost thousands of dollars and might not
satisfy federal authorities. Another alternative might be to move
the unfinished house, at heavy cost to Jones. Or Jones could sue
the county zoning administrator and the county commissioners
for permitting him, in good faith, to proceed at considerable cost
with the building. As Jones pondered this last possibility, he was
aware that two of the county commissioners were members of his
church. He recognized that the zoning administrator and the
commissioners were trying to do their job conscientiously.

Questions

1. Do you think a lawsuit is justified in any of the four cases?

2. What alternatives to a lawsuit do each of the four aggrieved
parties have?

The Laws of Evidence: Two or Three Witnesses

*A single witness may not give evidence against a man in the
matter of any crime or sin which he commits: a charge must be established on the evidence of two or of three witnesses.*

*When a malicious witness comes forward to give false evi-
dence against a man, and the two disputants stand before the
Lord, before the priests and the judges then in office, if, after
careful examination by the judges, he be proved to be a false witness giving false evidence against his fellow, you shall treat him as
he intended to treat his fellow, and thus rid yourselves of this*

wickedness. The rest of the people when they hear of it will be afraid: never again will anything as wicked as this be done among you. You shall show no mercy: life for life, eye for eye, tooth for tooth, hand for hand, foot for foot. (Deuteronomy 19:15-21)

Questions
1. Why are two or three witnesses more reliable than one?
2. Is eye-for-eye justice a limitation on harsher forms of retribution? Compare this with New Testament passages.

4.
Plagued by Harassing Neighbors

Everyone has encountered a bully who makes life miserable for others. Many also know ill-tempered persons who cannot be avoided. But few of us have endured as painful an experience as did the couple whose story is reported here. This case study includes a complex mix of issues—race, alcohol, emotional illness, and the law—and the role of police, professional and church friends. One senses that the Quintelas have drawn on strength from within and support from others in coping with their problem.

In 1980 an unpleasant crisis struck the young family of Alberto and Helen Quintela at their new home in St. Paul, Minnesota. Helen is a blond, blue-eyed daughter of a South Carolina Methodist family grounded in Southern values and traditions. Alberto is a dark-skinned, Spanish-speaking man who grew up in a migrant farm family of eight children in Carlsbad, New Mexico.

Alberto's family was poor. As children Alberto and his sisters worked with their parents, chopping and picking cotton and doing other farm work. They attended a Pentecostal Church, where Alberto's father, grandfather, and two uncles were preachers. Alberto's parents encouraged him, the only son in the family, to pursue an education. There were only laboring people in this Hispanic community—no doctors, lawyers, policemen, or teachers. A gifted high school student, Alberto attended a summer program at Carleton College in Minnesota. After his family moved to California he entered Claremont College and later transferred to Fresno Pacific College, a Mennonite Brethren school. While there, he served as a deacon and lay preacher in the local Pentecostal Church.

Alberto received a scholarship to the Harvard Graduate School of Education and became a part of the Harvard Mennonite Fellowship. There he met Helen, who had gone to Harvard to pursue a career. Despite initial reservations, Helen's parents approved of the marriage of their strong-willed daughter to this son of Hispanic farm laborers. The couple was married in a traditional formal ceremony after both attained master's degrees.

Alberto had been accepted by the Harvard Law School, the Harvard Divinity School, and the Harvard School of International Law. But he and Helen chose to move west to the University of Minnesota, where he could pursue a degree in corporate law, a field rarely entered by blacks or Hispanics. They lived in a small Minnesota town, where Helen taught fifth grade, Alberto attended law school, and both were active in a Mennonite Brethren church. Alberto, sensing a call to help his Hispanic people develop a strong economic and professional base, led in the establishment of the Minnesota Hispanic Chamber of Commerce. After graduation he obtained his first job in the Attorney General's office of the state of Minnesota. Then Helen and Alberto made two important decisions: first, to move into the inner city where they could be part of Alberto's people in a mixed white-Hispanic neighborhood on the West Side of St. Paul, and second, to become members of Faith Mennonite Church in Minneapolis.

Alberto now tells their story:

  ° ° ° ° °

I was on the top of the world. A top-notch lawyer with a law degree in business. My first job, my first home, expecting our first child. A new church where we knew the members and they knew us. A new neighborhood where we could help strengthen the Hispanic community. We planted our first garden. It was idyllic. An American dream. And then our world crashed in.

We moved next to a family that was ill in many ways. The father was a successful contractor but an alcoholic. His wife was also an alcoholic. They had three teenage sons who worked for their father but were into drugs, and three daughters who had behavioral problems as well. Two of the children had been in juvenile homes.

The family behavior seemed to go through cycles. The year we moved into the neighborhood the family was on a downward slide—just disintegrating. They began to exhibit all kinds of violent behavior, both physical and verbal. From sunup to sundown they were at each other's throats, cursing and fighting each other. We would sit down to dinner and not ten yards from our window a fist-fight would be going on. It was difficult not to let that affect us. It was like living next to hell. I would go to work and would hear fighting next door. I would come home tired, tense from a day at court, and there was all that turmoil next door. My wife, who was pregnant and at home throughout the day, became a prisoner of this vicious world. It was as though they had moved in with us. They were with us while we ate, while we watched TV, when we went to bed. They would throw a party every night until two or three in the morning, their friends screeching up to the house in their cars after work for a night of free drinks—yelling and cursing.

We talked to our neighbors and our friends. I decided, "I'm going to talk to this neighbor." I rehearsed my speech. One day I got up the nerve to talk to him. I knocked on the door. When the neighbor came to the door, I said: "For a couple of months we have been living next door. We like our house. My wife is pregnant. I have a job where I have to get up pretty early. I hate to be complaining, but could you speak to your kids about—?"

He broke in with a string of curses and exploded: "Who in hell do you think you are?" I started to explain, "Well, I just came over. . . ." He broke in again: "I've been living here seventeen years. If you don't like the way we're living, you can get out. I was here first. Just because you're an attorney and think you're a big shot, you think you can come in here and tell me what to do. Get the hell off my property." When a six-foot, 250-pound man tells you that, you scat.

I said to myself, "Maybe if a couple of us go." I talked with several neighbors. They said, "Yes, it is a problem, but there is not much we can do. Maybe we can have a parents' meeting on the block and invite the parents next door." But when we had a meeting and invited them, they did not come.

We asked the West Side Citizens Organization for assistance. We also asked the police liaison officer and community worker for help. The first time we mentioned the family's name, the police officer commented: "Not a chance. This guy has the worst record around. He's got a record a mile long. Nothing we can do except shoot 'em." I said, "Well, I'm a Mennonite and we don't believe in shooting. Isn't there anything else we can do?"

We talked to a Victim Crisis Center. They came to our home and interviewed us. They then went and interviewed our neighbors. The fellow came back and, as mad as he could be, said, "Well, I suggest you get a machine gun." I said, "Hey, wait, we don't believe in machine guns. Sure, this is a terrible situation, but I don't think guns will do any good."

At that point the family next door decided to build a party house behind their house. Then not only their family was partying there but also their friends. We had a tavern in our own backyard with not only four kids but fifteen to twenty. By this time they were aware that my wife and I were trying to do something about the situation and they began to turn their anger, hurts, and pain toward us. They began to harass us by yelling at me when I walked out of the house in the morning.

That winter we had joined Faith Mennonite Church. With the pastor we discussed how one witnesses at the point of conflict. Do you say: "I don't want to fight you. There is no point in fighting. Christ loves you." What do you do? I was scared. I would get off work, get off the bus, and as I would turn the corner they would be sitting there on their fence, drinking beer, and yelling at me: "You . . . faggot, I see you're home now. . . ."

It was like that, day in and day out. The police told us, "There's nothing we can do unless you want to press charges. Nothing we can do unless the community wants to do something." Nobody wanted to talk to the neighbors. Meanwhile, my Hispanic friends were becoming aware of the situation. It was very difficult to hide it from friends who came to dinner while there was a party going on next door. My friends would say, "Joe just got out of prison for killing someone. Just give us the word. You don't have to go through this. We can assign a bodyguard to go with you to work, to pick you up in the evening." I responded: "I appreciate your offer but I have officially become a Mennonite. We don't believe in violence. The love of Christ overcomes anything. We can overcome this family, too. They're a very disturbed family. They need love, they really do." The summer of 1980 closed on a very sour note, but it closed. Winter set in and our first child, Joseph, was born.

The bitter cold winter drove their parties inside. We heard no arguing. Helen's parents came to be with us. We were afraid to tell them what was going on next door. We felt a little guilty, a little afraid, a little ashamed. We didn't say much about it at church, either.

In the spring the old things started up again: screaming, shouting, yelling, cursing, fighting, and all the cars. We found it difficult to eat or sleep. We tried again the first cycle: talking to the neighbors, talking to community and citizen organizations, talking to the state legislator—a good friend of mine—and talking to the mayor, who was also a good friend.

I had become involved with a Hispanic action organization on the West Side. My Hispanic friends said, "The only way to deal with this problem is to fight fire with fire, violence with violence. You are not going to be able to win them over." I said, "What happens? I beat someone up, then they beat me up. Then three of you get together and beat someone up. . . . Someone pulls a gun."

In April 1981 the turmoil boiled over. A gang of kids decided to crash a party next door. They banged on the door and were refused entry. A riot almost took off. I awoke about 1:00 a.m. and saw three people in our backyard. I turned on our backyard lights. There was my neighbor and others in a fistfight. Two police cars pulled up and two policemen attempted to break up the fight. More police arrived. Our garden was trampled and the fence we had built that spring was smashed to bits. One of the kids with a knife had attempted to stab a police officer. A police officer pulled a gun and the riot was quieted. An officer knocked on the door and inquired, "Any damage done here? We're going to arrest these individuals for disorderly conduct and assault. You could also charge them with criminal destruction of property. Do you want to sign a complaint?" I looked out on our backyard and said, "Officer, no." Our neighbor came home at that point and started yelling at me: "You—talking to the police! You're not going to charge my kids with anything because when you do, I'm going to bash your head in the next time I see you." The police officer said, "We could arrest him too." I answered, "No, that's okay. We'll try to handle this in our own way."

Three days later, those who had been charged with disorderly conduct and then jailed were back. Another party began next door. Our son had undergone minor surgery earlier that day. Finally, Helen said, "Joseph can't sleep and I have taken this long enough. I'm going to call them and tell them to stop this." She picked up the phone and when she asked for the wife, she received a tongue-lashing from the other end of the line: "You put us in jail. Who the hell do you think you are?" My wife explained that we had just brought our son home from the hospital and would appreciate some quiet. I heard cursing on the phone. Helen responded, "We're just asking for peace and quiet." The voice at the other end shouted, "If you are a man just come out here and fight man to man. I've been here eighteen years. And if you don't come out here, I'm going to come over there."

Fifteen minutes later there was banging on the door. Then I amazed myself. I looked out, opened the door and walked out on the front porch to meet one of the sons. I said, "Mike, why don't you settle down? Let's just talk this thing out." This kid was yelling at me with two or three guys behind him also yelling and waving their fists. I said, "Hey, I'm not going to fight you. It's something I don't do. If you want to fight, well go ahead. I can't do that. I love you as a person. I love you as a friend, as a neighbor. I'm a Christian and a Mennonite. I'm not going to fight you but I would like you to be quiet." The guys behind him were screaming and yelling. I looked down the street and saw a police car rounding the corner. They saw the commotion and jumped out. The officer asked, "Mr. Quintela, is this guy bothering you?" I said, "Well, we were talking." The policeman grabbed him and threw him down.

Things went from bad to worse: April, May, June, July. I don't think we would have survived had it not been for our church. We finally turned to our church for help in April, saying: "We've got a problem that we can't handle on our own. We're going to be true to what we believe in. We need your help and support." My Hispanic friends kept saying, "Say the word, man, and we'll blow them away." I kept saying, "I can't do that." The church arranged for a support system, families coming in to pray with us.

In May we were having a picnic in our backyard after a terrible confrontation next door. Helen saw one of the sons coming over to us and thought he meant to apologize. She invited him over into our yard. He whaled into me: "Who do you think you are?" I sat there looking at him. He reached over and grabbed me by my throat and tried to pull me up. I remember saying, "Gary, this isn't going to solve anything. You have anger in you for some reason. Why are you angry at me?" He was infuriated that I wouldn't fight back. Helen jumped up and ran over to the neighbors to find his parents. A friend of his came over and said, "Gary, what's going on?" That crisis passed. On July 4 there was another major ruckus. The whole neighborhood complained. About twenty people were arrested. One of the sons threatened the police and us with a shotgun.

Our church decided to have Sunday vigils in our home. This brought the church and our family together. We shared meals and prayed together. As we heard the commotion outside we'd try to find peace with ourselves, in Christ, in the Word. In July our church decided to have a twenty-four hour, seven-day-a-week candlelight vigil and worship service in our home as an expression of nonviolent response to violence. Not only did church members participate but also members of our community and other acquaintances. The local newspaper got wind of it. People signed up for eight hour shifts to live with us, 8:00 a.m. to 3:00 p.m., 3:00 to 11:00 p.m., 10:30 p.m. to 8:00 a.m. People were coming in all the time. Others would ask, "What's going on here? What are all these cars doing in front of your house?" "Our friends are Mennonites," we explained. "They believe in nonviolence. They believe we can conquer." During all of this our church became one.

In the middle of our vigil on July 27 someone looked out the window and said, "Something terrible has happened to your car." All the tires had been punctured. I took the car to the service station. The attendant saw the punctured tires and asked me, "You the family over on Baker Street having all those problems?" "Yes," I said. "I want to give you a set of new tires," he told me.

In August I accepted an invitation to attend the national convention of the U.S. Chamber of Commerce in Kansas City. One morning at three o'clock I received a phone call in my hotel room from Helen. She told me: "Our house has been firebombed. Our garage has been burned down. I'm okay. Joseph is okay. You should come home as quickly as you can." I picked up the phone and called my closest friend, a state representative, and said: "Frank, I want you to go over and support my wife." I also called the president of the Minnesota section of the Hispanic Congress and called the director of the West Side Citizens Organization. Within fifteen minutes Frank, Wib, and Ralph showed up at our home. Before they left, however, they called two or three others, who called two or three, who called two or three. Between four in the morning and four in the afternoon we had at least two hundred people from all sections of the community come to our home. By the time I returned home that afternoon we had an outpouring of support—everybody from the mayor to a state senator, practically half of our church, the whole Hispanic Chamber of Commerce, Hispanic organizations, and all kinds of other people.

When I arrived, some fifty people in our house were all arguing whether or not they should go after the people next door. Some people were praying upstairs; some were praying in the kitchen. People coming in. People bringing food in. We had a campout.

We moved out of our home, our first home. We're still a part of the neighborhood and have become a symbol in our community. Love can conquer all. The community knows me as the lawyer who believes in nonviolence and, whenever I have been asked to intervene in a situation, a nonviolent unit has been created in that community. Faith Mennonite Church, my church, has decided to do evangelism in the community because we have such a residue of people who have read newspaper accounts of our story. I wouldn't be where I am now without having had a supportive group of people. They say, "We believe in what you believe. The trouble and turmoil we went through served as an inspiration to families in our church to take their own steps and to stand up for what they believe in. Trust in the Lord and he will see you through."

I think of that neighbor family as a runaway train. Their home met their needs for socializing, action, attention. They were free in that house to let their emotions out, to escape into fantasy, to drink, and to be as violent as they wanted. For them this house was their turf and they made the rules for their territory. Friends could come and have all the drink they wanted and could escape with them to their fantasy world.

We had mixed feelings as to whether we should bring suit against our neighbors. When we calculated the financial costs of leaving that house, we found that we had suffered costs which ran into tens of thousands of dollars. We discussed what we should have done differently. We knew that we had made many mistakes. We asked for prayers of others that we might learn and grow from this terrible and beautiful experience.

Questions
1. What key values underlie Helen and Alberto's actions?
2. Was Alberto's decision to confront his troublesome neighbor wise? Would there have been other ways of dealing with the neighbor family?
3. Should the Quintelas have moved out of the neighborhood when the situation became difficult, instead of waiting and trying to deal with it?
4. Did the Quintelas' commitment to nonviolence fail or succeed?

Seek Help When the Conflict Is Too Difficult

When the issue in any lawsuit is beyond your competence, whether it be a case of blood against blood, plea against plea, or blow against blow, that is disputed in your courts, then go up without delay to the place which the Lord your God will choose. There you must go to the levitical priests or to the judge then in office; seek their guidance, and they will pronounce the place which the Lord will choose. See that you carry out all their instructions. Act on the instruction which they give you, or on the precedent that they cite; do not swerve from what they tell you, either to right or to left. Anyone who presumes to reject the decision either of the priest who ministers there to the Lord your God, or of the judge, shall die; thus you will rid Israel of wickedness. Then all the people will hear of it and be afraid, and will never again show such presumption. (Deuteronomy 17:8-13)

Questions

1. When may a conflict be too difficult for one   person to handle?
2. To whom can one go for help?

5.
The Picked-on Child Tries to Cope

Almost every school has children who are "picked on" by their peers. The ways of "picking on" a classmate are infinitely varied—from persistent teasing to name-calling and taunting, from pestering and goading to browbeating, from threatening and intimidation to physical violence. The reasons for such harassment may relate to physical weakness or handicaps, to racial, ethnic, religious or socioeconomic status, or to personality traits. The reasons why children torment certain of their peers are also varied: envy, insecurity, an impulse to dominate. The picked-on child may endure without the knowledge of teachers or parents and may try a variety of methods to elude his or her annoying peers. The child must struggle with issues of alienation, rejection, and conflict resolution that would be perplexing even for an adult.

Following are several cases told by adults as they recall their own experiences or those of their peers in coping with the unfriendly behavior of classmates.

a. Acting as Though He Had Heard Nothing

Armin Wiebe, in the novel *The Salvation of Yasch Siemens,* tells a fictional story which may have its roots in a true story: A boy named Emmanuel Rempel went to the Gutenthal, Manitoba, community to live with his grandmother. He immediately found friends in the sixth grade. Forscha, however, seemed to take an instant dislike to Emmanuel. Forscha and a few of his gang galloped as horsemen through a group playing ball, grabbed the ball and threw it away. Emmanuel said nothing when Forscha bothered them; he waited until Forscha ran away and then began again to play. When Emmanuel and his friends played Flying Dutchman or Last Couple Out, Forscha and his gang tried to break up the game. Emmanuel did not become angry; he just waited until they went away.

After recess, when the students from the upper grades were reading aloud from the Bible, one read something about Emmanuel. Forscha raised his hand and asked what Emmanuel meant. The teacher said, "It means Jesus. That was his name before he was born." After school Forscha taunted Emmanuel with the word "Jesus." His gang laughed. On other occasions when Emmanuel appeared, Forscha and his gang said "Here comes Jesus" or sang "Jesus loves me, this I know." Once when Emmanuel was in the privy Forscha's gang stood around it and sang, "Jesus puts his money in the Bank of Montreal—Jesus saves, Jesus saves, Jesus saves." Emmanuel emerged, acting as though he had heard nothing.

Walking Away from Trouble

But the Pharisees, on leaving the synagogue, laid a plot to do away with him. Jesus was aware of it and withdrew. (Matthew 12:14-15)

At these words the whole congregation were infuriated. They leapt up, threw him out of the town, and took him to the brow of the hill on which it was built, meaning to hurl him over the edge. But he walked straight through them all, and went away. (Luke 4:28-30)

Question
When is it prudent to walk away from conflict?

b. *A College Student Tells His Story*

When I was in the second grade most of the country schools in our part of the state were closed and we were bussed to town schools. Country kids were different from town kids. We got into fights. These fights escalated for me into one major conflict over the next nine years.

By the time I entered high school there was nothing I could do about the situation. People would say, "Let's beat up Schmidt" for no reason other than my being a country kid or that they wanted to prove their superiority. But somehow in the midst of this I picked up pacifistic ideas. My pacifism was rooted in practical necessity. At any moment there might be only one person beating me up, but I knew that if I fought back I'd immediately have ten ganging up on me. My personality and my refusal to fight back just seemed to encourage people to beat me up.

I didn't want to go to school. School was hell. I acted differently at home than at school since home was refuge from hell, a place of emotional release. My dad never understood my plight. He wanted me to stick it out at school. He said that as the older students graduated and left school my situation would improve. I knew better than to believe that. Students younger than me were beating me up. To beat me had become an accepted cultural pattern in our school. I felt there was nothing I could do and there was no one to intervene in my behalf.

During the summer between my sophomore and junior years in high school, I was invited to attend a church camp of another Mennonite group. Here I was free from the oppression and constant abuse I experienced in high school. For the first time in my life I was accepted as I was. I decided that I wanted to stay with these neat people I had met at camp, many of whom attended a nearby parochial school.

In our church most people considered that church school a bad place, the work of the devil. But I found that I could live with those people and not with the ones in my own public high school.

It was difficult to convince my parents to let me attend the other school. They wanted me to try our public high school "just one more time" to see if it would be better. But I knew it would never change and that I could not survive two more years there. One night, in a burst of emotion I cried out, "I'm sick and tired of going through hell every day at school." I don't think my parents understood.

But they finally accepted the fact that I was not going back to the public school. They never gave me permission to go to the church school, but neither did they say I could not go; I just went. The situation at our high school had deteriorated to the point where there was only one thing left that I could do and that was to run. I ran.

At the church school I underwent a sudden and dramatic transformation. For the first time in my life I was free. I was accepted as a human being. For the first time I enjoyed, really enjoyed, school. Life was fun. In time I had conflicts at the church school but that is a different story.

Getting Rid of a Disagreeable Person

Joseph had a dream; and when he told it to his brothers, they hated him still more. . . . They saw him in the distance, and before he reached them, they plotted to kill him. They said to each other, "Here comes that dreamer. Now is our chance; let us kill him and throw him into one of these pits and say that a wild beast has devoured him. Then we shall see what will come of his dreams." When Reuben heard, he came to his rescue, urging them not to take his life. "Let us have no bloodshed," he said. "Throw him into this pit in the wilderness, but do him no bodily harm." He meant to save him from them so as to restore him to his father. (Genesis 37:5, 18-22)

Question

What are acceptable ways of coping with the obnoxious behavior of an arrogant person?

c. *An Older Man Recalls His Boyhood*

In grade school I ranked as one of the better pupils in my class. As years passed, some of the brightest students in the grade moved away, leaving me at the top of our class. I was the next youngest member of the class. The youngest, the second-best student in the class, was my close neighbor and daily playmate.

In the seventh grade I began to feel intense competition from my playmate. He always wanted to know what grade I'd received and when he received a better grade he told others. He pretended that he didn't need to study but would sneak books home to study in an effort to get a higher grade. When we played football or baseball on the schoolyard, he singled out my mistakes for criticism. I was particularly annoyed when he called me by my last name on the playground while all the rest called me by my nickname. If I retaliated by calling him by his last name, he only used my last name more frequently. He knew he was getting under my skin. I thought my playmate's mother was overly competitive and needled him into being annoyingly aggressive. So, all along, I blamed her for his behavior.

My teacher observed this unhealthy competition. He encouraged me to take the eighth-grade state examinations "for the fun of it." I did, and scored at the top of the eighth-grade class. He spoke to my parents about the unpleasant rivalry and encouraged them to permit me to skip the eighth grade to escape this situation. This I did. I entered high school at the age of twelve, about a year and half younger than the other students. From that time on, my neighbor and I went separate ways, but we kept in touch with each other through the years. We have both pursued careers in human relations fields. Our competitive attitudes toward each other have faded. However, we have never discussed the painful rivalries of our boyhood years.

d. *A Young Mother Describes her School Years.*

I was the picked-on one in high school. We lived on a farm two miles from town. A cousin of mine, one month older than me, was the leader of a group of eight girls in our class. I was excluded from all organizations and clubs to which one was elected. I had a low image of myself through four years of high school. I sought escape by sleeping and eating, and weighed as much as 180 pounds. My parents did not know how to help me achieve recognition. Achievement among classmates related to good looks, popularity, and attention from boys. I engaged in some forms of negative behavior to get attention. Suicide was extremely uncommon among high school students. I never considered it.

I went to our church college after high school as did my cousin. There I was less under her domination. I remember the turning point. I attended a funeral service in which the pastor, citing Scripture, declared that "the last shall be first and the first shall be last." It dawned on me that one didn't have to wait until heaven for that to happen. It could happen now. I was not changed abruptly, but I started struggling. I realized that if I was patient, my time would come.

I transferred to another church college for my sophomore year. Over a period of six months I lost sixty pounds. I was completely free from that high school group of eight girls. Then my cousin transferred to my college and wanted to room with me. Mother said I should not agree. I said I could handle it now. My cousin tried to reassert her domination but I was on my way to discovering independence and self-worth. She stayed for only three months. Eventually she went to a school of cosmetology, got married, and settled down in the community with her husband and three children. She is the secretary for our high school class and organized the tenth reunion. Those high school years are still the golden era for her. We write to each other occasionally, but we don't have much in common. I have no desire to talk with her about those unhappy high school experiences.

I can look back now on those experiences and see them as positive for me. I married later than others and found a spouse with whom I can make mutual decisions. My interests and values are different now, but I still have traces of that earlier insecurity.

Although I had planned to go to our tenth-year reunion, at the last moment I decided not to go. I wasn't prepared to be the new person that I now am. Maybe the next time I will go.

Questions

1. Discuss the college student's comment, "My refusal to fight back just seemed to encourage people to beat me up." Is it possible that at times nonviolence encourages violent response?

2. What counsel would you have given each picked-on child?

3. Do you know of cases in which persons are picked on? Are there lessons in their stories on how to cope?

Reconciliation

Then Joseph said to his brothers, "Come closer," and so they came close. He said, "I am your brother Joseph whom you sold into Egypt. Now do not be distressed to take it amiss that you sold me into slavery here; it was God who sent me ahead of you to save men's lives. For there have now been two years of famine in the country, and there will be another five years with neither ploughing nor harvest. . . . Give [my father] this message . . . :

" 'You shall live in the land of Goshen and be near me, you, your sons and your grandsons, your flocks and herds and all that you have. I will take care of you there, you and your household and all that you have, and see that you are not reduced to poverty; there are still five years of famine to come.' You can see for yourselves, and so can my brother Benjamin, that it is Joseph himself who is speaking to you. Tell my father of all the honor which I enjoy in Egypt, tell him all you have seen, and make haste to bring him down here." Then he threw his arms round his brother Benjamin and wept, and Benjamin too embraced him weeping. He kissed all his brothers and wept over them, and afterwards his brothers talked with him. (Genesis 45:4-6; 10-15)

Questions

What problems did Joseph have in accepting his brothers? What problems did the brothers have with Joseph?

Congregational

6.
Changing the Structures to Meet the Needs

The New Testament, like the Old Testament, candidly describes the pettiness, meanness, and quarreling among people, even among the followers of Jesus. At times some of the early Christian leaders were difficult to live with. The following is an elaboration of a conflict that occurred in the first Christian congregation, as recorded in Acts 6:1-7.

In Jerusalem, Christians established the first congregation. This may have occurred only a few days after Jesus' resurrection and ascension. Members of this congregation were Jews who had known Jesus intimately. None would ever forget the events of that last week: the triumphal entry into Jerusalem; the encounter with the profiteers in the temple; the final teaching sessions together; the evening dinner; the defection of Judas; the arrest in the garden; the trial, sentence, and agonizing death on the cross; the despair of the day after; Jesus' appearance to the women at the tomb, to the two disciples on the road, and to the small group; and finally his departure into heaven. The old city was alive with memories of the lost leader. Members of the first congregation could take persons on a walking tour of Jerusalem and could point out countless places that triggered memories of Jesus' presence.

Many in this Christian congregation appeared to be Jewish in their social practices, language, food, and clothing. The congregation radiated a spirit that led people to want to be part of the fellowship, and soon began to draw many new members. Not all were natives of Jerusalem. Some were immigrants from a distance who spoke Greek. They were not accustomed to traditional Hebrew practices.

The word of the spectacular growth of the Jerusalem congregation spread to people of various cultures scattered in distant cities around the Mediterranean. Thrilled with the news of this enthusiastic Christian community, friends from a distance sent gifts to support the new congregation's evangelism and church planting program.

Many viewed the Jerusalem group as the model Christian congregation. Thus they expressed shock when they heard complaining from within the congregation. The new Christians, who recently had come from a distance to Jerusalem, grumbled that they felt like outsiders. Some protested, "We are treated like second-class citizens." Some newcomers arrived in Jerusalem without money, jobs, or places to live. The new arrivals complained: "Just because we speak Greek and not the local Aramaic we suffer from discrimination. Those of us who are poor— widows, orphans, others in real need—are overlooked when church leaders distribute relief gifts from abroad."

The new members became bold: "We thought in a Christian fellowship we would find equality: share and share alike. If we had good Jewish names, had relatives in the congregation, and had grown up practicing the old Hebrew customs, we would be treated more fairly. And the leaders call themselves 'followers of Jesus.' "

Their protests soon reached the ears of members of the board of apostles, known as "the twelve." They acknowledged, "We have been so absorbed in sending out preaching teams and instructing the new believers that we have neglected some important tasks." The twelve invited the unhappy church members to meet with them and to share their complaints and concerns. The twelve listened attentively, apologized for failing to be sensitive to their needs, and promised to act promptly.

The twelve discussed possible solutions, one being that they themselves would manage the welfare-distribution program. But they realized that since they were already carrying a full load, they should turn to other congregational members with the gifts to administer the welfare program.

The twelve called a congregational meeting. They proposed that seven respected persons should be selected to serve as a committee to care for needy members. The assembly approved the plan and nominated seven persons. Among those chosen for this committee were several from the "outsider" group. The congregation then held a commissioning service with singing, prayer, and words of encouragement for the new committee.

The Jerusalem congregation continued to grow and to share the good news of Jesus. Within the congregation were those who said: "Those complaints were painful to hear. We had thought that we were one big, happy family. However, those unhappy members helped us to become the kind of congregation that Jesus would want us to be."

Questions

1. How can complaints be used to strengthen the quality of life in a congregation?

2. What steps were taken by the Jerusalem congregation to resolve the conflict?

3. What happens to a congregation that ignores or discourages complaints from its members?

Forgive as the Lord Forgave You

Then put on the garments that suit God's chosen people, his own, his beloved: compassion, kindness, humility, gentleness, patience. Be forbearing with one another, and forgiving, where any of you has cause for complaint: you must forgive as the Lord forgave you. To crown all, there must be love, to bind all together and complete the whole. Let Christ's peace be arbiter in your hearts; to this peace you were called as members of a single body. And be filled with gratitude. (Colossians 3:12-15)

Questions

1. Are these attitudes matters of will or skill?
2. How can these qualities be acquired?

7.
An Angry Man Confronts the Deacons

A person who explodes with anger can evoke varied reactions: fear and flight, ridicule, or even a counter outburst of anger. If we are to live with other people, we must learn to handle our anger and the anger of others. We also need to learn when and how to intervene in angry conflicts, even when help is spurned.

In recent years separations and divorces have increased among members of our congregations. Some feel that family, friends, and church members should stay out of marital conflicts. But in the Christian church, when one member suffers, all suffer. The following case study explores ways of helping when previous offers of assistance have been rejected.

Ann Smith married James King in Grace Church, where they were both members. Ann was nineteen and James, twenty. Seven months after the wedding their child, Allen, was born. From the beginning they had difficulties in their marriage. They attended Sunday morning worship services but rarely participated in other activities. Their circle of friends was outside the congregation. Eventually, the couple moved to a nearby town where they occasionally attended a church where James had once been a member.

Two and a half years after their wedding, Ann met Jeff Clark at a drive-in restaurant where she worked. Jeff, who was in his late twenties, had held a number of short-term jobs and had served briefly in the army. Jeff was proud of this experience and talked of it often. Ann was attracted to Jeff and to his aggressive, confident ways.

Ann's parents, who were active in Grace Church, were deeply concerned about Ann and Jim and their deteriorating marriage. They talked to Ann frequently but found that she resisted their efforts. Her parents encouraged church friends to maintain contact with Ann and Jim. The pastor spoke with Ann and Jim several times and found some openness for counsel, especially on the part of Jim. Several congregational members sought opportunities to talk with Ann, who had grown up in the church. She was open to talking about her marriage and at the end of each visit thanked them for their concern.

Ann, however, left Jim. She sued for divorce and requested custody of Allen. During the divorce proceedings two women members of the board of deacons talked to Ann on separate occasions. Each expressed her concern for Ann and Jim and offered to help Ann think through the issues. Throughout the pending divorce Jim stated his interest in preserving the marriage and reestablishing it on firmer ground. But Ann did not want to discuss the issues with the pastor or either of the two deacons. She politely stated there was no hope for saving the marriage.

One evening twelve members of the board of deacons of Grace Church were holding a monthly meeting at the church when the pastor was called out of the session. Fifteen minutes later he returned to the room with a young man dressed in a khaki army jacket. The newcomer's face was grim and he seemed distraught. The pastor, standing in the doorway, apologized for the interruption and stated, "This is Jeff Clark. We have been talking and he would like to say something to the board of deacons." Several members of the board were well acquainted with the case of Ann, Jim, and Jeff, although no one knew Jeff personally. Some knew very little about the situation.

Jeff came immediately to the point: "In a month Ann's divorce will be final. Church members have no right to butt into her personal affairs. This is her decision. In other churches members don't interfere in personal matters like this." The pastor explained his role in making himself available to Ann and Jim, as well as the congregation's concern for all marriages. Jeff repeated his demand that the church stay out of the situation, and continued to speak in angry bursts. The pastor asked occasional questions to help Jeff make clear what he wanted to say. Jeff granted that the pastor might have a right to talk to Ann but that deacons and other members of the church had no such right.

The members of the board sat silently as Jeff poured out his feelings. Jeff challenged them to say something. He declared he would defend his rights with a gun. He asserted that he was no coward and would fight for his country, stating, "If it weren't for people like me who are ready to fight for our country, you couldn't worship here."

The level of tension in the room remained high as Jeff repeated that church members should "butt out" of what he declared were private concerns. One of the women spoke quietly and directly to him, explaining how she had tried to be helpful to Ann and Jim. She told him that she had expressed congregational concern in reaching out to Ann. "We do care as a congregation," she stated. Another board member spoke calmly to Jeff, outlining how she had sought to relate to Ann in a caring way. She said that she had not seen these as acts of interference but as efforts to be friendly and helpful. She said that she regretted it if she had offended Ann.

After the two women spoke, Jeff remained silent. He then explained that Ann didn't like the pressure everyone was putting on her and repeated his demand that the church not interfere. The pastor responded that he and the church did not wish to interfere but wanted to be helpful. After half an hour Jeff shook hands with the pastor and left the room.

When the board reconvened after a short break, they reviewed the half-hour session and agreed that Jeff probably felt that he had discouraged any further efforts of the church to contact Ann. The pastor reported that Ann's parents had tried in many ways to help Ann and Jim but that Ann seemed to resist all their efforts. Several board members spoke of the power of prayer. Others emphasized that parents and the congregation sometimes have to recognize their limitations in exerting influence.

For the next hour the board discussed what the pastor or individual deacons could do which would be helpful and not injurious. They asked a variety of questions: "How much should we honor Jeff's demand that the church stay out of it?" "Did Jeff really speak for Ann?" "Jeff acknowledged with reluctance the role of the pastor. Should the pastor take the next step in seeing Ann and perhaps Jim?" "Should one of the deacon women try to meet with Ann, despite Jeff's demand that further 'butting in' be stopped?" "Are there other people who can be helpful?"

A month later the divorce was granted with custody for Allen divided between the two parents. Neither Ann nor Jim had been in church for a long time. Ann and Jeff were making plans to be married.

Questions

1. Discuss Jeff's assertion that "church members have no right to butt into [other people's] personal affairs." When is a church helpful and when is it meddlesome?

2. Imagine yourself as a deacon, present in the room when Jeff confronted the group. How would you have responded to him?

Make Friends with Your Accuser

You have learned that our forefathers were told, "Do not commit murder; anyone who commits murder must be brought to judgement." But what I tell you is this: Anyone who nurses anger against his brother must be brought to judgement. If he abuses his brother he must answer for it to the court; if he sneers at him he will have to answer for it in the fires of hell.

If, when you are bringing your gift to the altar, you suddenly remember that your brother has a grievance against you, leave your gift where it is before the altar. First go and make your peace with your brother, and only then come back and offer your gift.

If someone sues you, come to terms with him promptly while you are both on your way to court; otherwise he may hand you over to the judge, and the judge to the constable, and you will be put in jail. (Matthew 5:21-25)

Questions
1. Why should one resolve a conflict as quickly as possible?
2. When is it better to be cautious and deliberate?

8.
A Congregation Responds to the Draft

Few issues set Quakers, Brethren, and Mennonites apart from their fellow citizens more than the issue of military service. Members of these historic peace churches are often torn by the appeals of nation and the urgings of their religious heritage.

One's love of country can collide with one's love of Christ. This often generates intense emotions. In the spirit of American individualism, many consider conscientious objection to be a solely personal decision. Yet some Christians, viewing the church as a caring fellowship, believe that the congregation can come to a common mind.

In January 1980, President Jimmy Carter, in response to the Soviet Union's invasion of Afghanistan, revived the requirement of draft registration for men at the age of eighteen. In central Kansas, the Salem Mennonite congregation sought to respond to this complex issue. The following is a summary of events at Salem Mennonite Church following the President's statement:

Early February 1980: Salem Mennonite sponsored a meeting for the church youth in response to President Carter's proposal. The meeting was organized by Salem's youth sponsor and Greg, a conference worker.

July 2: President Carter officially announced the renewal of mandatory draft registration of all nineteen- and twenty-year-old men. He signed a proclamation ordering the young men to register at post offices between July 21 and August 2.

July 16: At the 42nd triennial session of the General Conference in Estes Park, Colorado, six eighteen-year-old men, two of them from the Salem congregation, presented a statement explaining their decision not to register for the draft. The young men invited churchwide support for their position.

July 17: An ad hoc group, involving Greg from the Salem congregation, presented a statement to the conference assembly. Following discussion, a resolution was passed in support of the nonregistrants:

> As members of the General Conference Mennonite Church, meeting in conference at Estes Park, Colorado, on July 12-19, 1980, we have been gifted by God to hear a statement by our draft-age youth of their deep conscience against registering with the U.S. Selective Service. As gathered members of the body of Jesus Christ, we reaffirm our 1971 General Conference statement on *The Way of Peace* and support the findings of the 1980 MCC Assembly on the draft. These express our historic support for the conscience of these persons as well as for those whose conscientious decision is to register in anticipation of alternative service consistent with their Christian witness. Here and now we, as Canadian and U.S. members of the General Conference Mennonite Church, state our intention to walk with these persons and all peacemakers who give sole loyalty to Jesus Christ. We shall support them personally, spiritually, and financially in their costly witness, and shall stand by them publicly, in courts of law, in jail if necessary, or as emigrants, should they so choose. . . .

July 21: Draft registration of all nineteen- and twenty-year-old men began at U.S. post offices. A group sympathetic to conscientious objectors staged a brief demonstration at the local post office.

July 23: Salem's youth sponsors initiated and led a Wednesday evening interchurch meeting. Deacons, church leaders, and many draft-age youth were present. Participants raised several issues: Should youth register, or refuse to register? How much support should the congregation give to nonregistrants? What are appropriate expressions of witness to the community? The group discussed several options, including support of nonregistrants from other congregations, draft registration counseling, and publicizing support of nonregistrants.

July 27: Following the Sunday morning worship service, Ted, a draft-age youth who had recently joined Salem Mennonite, along with a father of two teenage sons, presented concerns to the congregation. The father introduced the nonregistration issue and invited a congregational response. Ted requested individuals in the congregation to sign an ad for the local newspaper declaring support.

Some congregational members expressed discomfort with the action. They were concerned that, by the lack of background information and the lack of clarity, this was an invitation to individuals rather than a call for a congregational decision. They asserted that church decision-making procedures had been bypassed. Some called for further discussion.

Late July: Sixty-five Mennonites from Salem and other area churches signed a statement of support for nonregistrants and conscientious objectors. The statement appeared in the local newspaper on July 26.

October 5: A Salem congregational meeting failed to address draft registration due to lack of time. A meeting was scheduled for October 19 to give full attention to the issue.

October 19: Approximately forty members, constituting a congregational quorum, attended the special meeting. A member of the board of deacons introduced the registration and draft issues and read the Estes Park affirmation. Several questions arose during the discussion.

(1) How can we support the statement but also express concern for those who are not conscientious objectors?

(2) Are we engaging in, or supporting, civil disobedience if we affirm this statement?

(3) Should we be cautious about actions which might alienate the community?

(4) What does it mean to give financial support?

(5) How are draft resisters demonstrating that their lives are committed to service? One person commented that alternative service is a stronger witness than nonregistration, while another said that cooperating with registration signifies too close a link to a structure of national coercion.

(6) Is the statement affirmed by the conference stronger than our own convictions, as, for example, the language of "sole loyalty" and "witness costs"?

Some felt that the Salem congregation should write its own statement. Although there had been forty present at the beginning, only twenty-one voted at the end of the meeting: sixteen for the resolution and five opposed. The others abstained.

October 21: The church council reviewed the meeting and decision of October 19. The validity of the earlier meeting was questioned on the grounds that a quorum was not present. The Council raised several other concerns: Is the attention given to this issue creating a negative reaction among some in the congregation? What messages are we giving to our youth by how we treat this issue? Finally, several felt that the vote did not adequately represent the congregation because of its small sampling.

October 26: During Sunday worship, a church council member reported to the congregation the current situation and suggested further discussion. The next congregational meeting was scheduled for February of 1981.

November 2: On Peace Sunday, the pastor addressed the congregation during worship. He stated: "I believe that we as a congregation should support those who take either response."

November 31: A Sunday school class for all ages began under the direction of Greg on the topic of draft and registration. Approximately a dozen attended the thirteen sessions.

By late fall, talk of nonregistration and the congregation's role had diminished. The conference had acted. The congregation had approved the conference action. Initially some in the church council may have been displeased. The pastor had affirmed his support for both those who registered as conscientious objectors and those who refused to register. A Sunday school class was meeting under the leadership of the author of the conference statement. Some felt the congregation should meet again to reconsider its October 19 action and to draft a substitute statement. Others preferred to let the situation rest. At least two young conscientious objectors of the congregation had not registered.

Seven persons in the church explained their perspectives on the issues:

Greg, the conference worker, was not a member of Salem but participated actively in the life of the congregation. Greg felt that the conflict might become a generational issue, with older members of the congregation siding with alternative service or conscientious objection, and draft-age youth and others tending towards nonregistration. Greg supported the nonregistrant position, but emphasized his role as a peacemaker. He also supported those who chose to register.

Greg felt that lack of information had contributed to threatening the security of certain persons in the church. He expressed his concern that the handling of the issue had introduced a certain element of "dishonesty, lack of trust, coercion, and manipulation." He felt that communication between various groups was still relatively open.

Ted, the young man who had spoken before the congregation on July 27, felt that one factor in the conflict was a lack of consensus on how to bring about social change. He called the situation "a battle between what's been done in the past that hasn't worked and what has to be done in the future." He stated that "it is the church's obligation both morally and spiritually" to support those who refuse to register because of conscience.

As a positive step, Ted suggested that the congregation draft a statement of its own. Ted blamed the older generation at Salem for not taking the issue seriously: "They took the easiest path to quiet the most voices. It's the apathy that bothers me. And there's too much bureaucracy. The church gave support reluctantly."

Salem's youth director sensed a conflict between those "who perceived draft and registration as it was ten to twenty years ago and those who have a more current view of militarism as evil." She identified the July 27 Sunday meeting as a major source of "pressure, tension, and discomfort" because the issue was presented with too little background and because the church leadership did not have direct involvement. She also noted the young people's absence at church meetings.

The youth director saw herself as a mediator on the issue. She described a need for further study and dialogue but claimed that "the tension until now has not been unwholesome." Although she pointed out that the church might agree on a new statement, "the issues of registration and the draft are only the tip of the iceberg in terms of lifestyle."

A *deacon* observed that the nonregistration issue evoked discomfort among some members. However, he noted that a number of members felt free to voice their concerns and that the congregation did act. He believed that better preparation—for example, dividing the meeting into small discussion groups— might have provided a better reception for the Estes statement. He questioned whether congregational opinion divided neatly along age lines: "I would guess that most of the sixteen voting for the Estes statement were forty-five years or older. I would guess, further, that the unspoken resistance to the Estes statement came from a minority who feel that the church should somehow affirm those who served in the military."

The church secretary felt that the issue had not been handled well. He indicated that some congregational members had a distorted perception of Salem's options. He suggested that many people had abstained from voting on the Estes resolution because of the clause regarding financial support, and because it failed to address those who approve of military participation.

A *longtime member* of the Salem congregation did not see the situation as a conflict but suggested that the events "may have pulled us closer together." As one of the five who voted against adopting the Estes resolution, he favored registration with con-scientious-objector status over nonregistration. He felt he could not make a commitment to support the nonregistrants financially, although he added, "I have no objection to prayerful support." He concluded, "Here at Salem there is such a thing as disagreeing agreeably."

The pastor believed that rather than a conflict, there were simply two positions needing clarification in the church: "We should recognize that both positions are conscientious-objector positions." He described the situation as "Christian people responding in different ways: both responses are Christian and valid. I would attempt to help people understand this. The danger is in thinking that one response is more Christian than the other. . . . There has been no damage. It has helped us to focus on an issue of pacifism that has to be dealt with."

The congregation's stand on nonregistration was not ad-dressed at the next congregational meeting. During the next months, though Salem Mennonite church members continued to discuss registration and nonregistration, open disagreement re-garding the issue diminished and people turned to other concerns.

Questions

1. Discuss Greg's feeling that lack of information had threatened the security of certain persons in the church. Can you design a process that would have made it easier to discuss these issues?

2. Do you agree with Ted that the conflict revealed a lack of consensus in the congregation on how to bring about social change? Have you witnessed a congregational conflict in which the division reflected the viewpoints of different age-groups?

3. Do you agree with the deacons' conclusion that "better prepara-tion" of the congregation might have improved the reception of the nonregistration issue?

4. Discuss the pastor's perspective that rather than a conflict there were simply two positions needing clarification in the church. Is it possi-ble for a congregation to discuss difficult or sensitive issues without caus-ing division?

Testing All Opinions and Statements

Do not stifle inspiration, and do not despise prophetic utterances, but bring them all to the test and then keep what is good in them and avoid the bad. . . .

But do not trust any and every spirit, my friends; test the spirits, to see whether they are from God. . . . (I Thessalonians 5:19-22; 1 John 4:1)

Questions

1. In a clash of opinions and declarations, what guidelines will test for the truth?

2. If you suspect someone of lying or distorting information, how can you probe in a caring spirit?

9.

The Covenant for Congregational Meetings

Some congregations are torn by partisan factions and emotionally heated meetings. It may appear to outsiders that they enjoy verbal conflict. This case study explores one way for congregations to grow in the art of disagreeing agreeably.

Peace Valley Baptist Church had more than its share of church conflicts: controversies included building an educational wing, paving the parking lot, adding air-conditioning, hiring a youth pastor, selecting choir music, calling and dismissing pastors. One member defended the congregation's reputation for angry arguments thus: "We take our church so seriously that on any issue we are ready to fight." Some in other churches called the congregation the "Battling Baptists."

A new pastor arrived who soon learned of his congregation's disposition to argue heatedly in church meetings. During the first year of his new pastorate he preached a series of four sermons on "The Church Militant and the Church Reconciling." In these sermons he reviewed the biblical teachings on how the church carries out its ministry while "having the mind and spirit of Christ." Many spoke appreciatively of the series, although a few admitted that at times they felt uncomfortable because the pastor seemed to be preaching directly to them.

In the final sermon, which came the week before the annual congregational meeting, he preached on Matthew 18:15-20. He said that since he had been asked to lead in prayer at the beginning and closing of the annual meeting, he planned prior to the meeting to distribute a slip of paper on which would be printed a "covenant." He planned to invite the congregation to read it after his opening prayer:

> We covenant with each other to receive with appreciation the reports shared in this meeting, to listen carefully to each other in love even when a differing point of view is expressed, to speak out of our own experience when appropriate, to search the Scriptures for guidance on issues, and to uphold this congregation in prayer, remembering that we are the body of Christ.

The pastor asked the members of his congregation to comment to him after the annual meeting as to whether reading the covenant had helped them to participate with the mind and spirit of Christ.

Questions

1. Was the new pastor wise in dealing directly with the congregation's reputation for controversy?

2. What kind of covenant (or set of "ground rules") might your congregation want to establish before its next congregational meeting? Would such a covenant be helpful?

Negotiating an Agreement

Now certain persons who had come down from Judaea began to teach the brotherhood that those who were not circumcised in accordance with Mosaic practice could not be saved. That brought them into fierce dissension and controversy with Paul and Barnabas. And so it was arranged that these two and some others from Antioch should go up to Jerusalem to see the apostles and elders about this question . . . .

When they reached Jerusalem they were welcomed by the church and the apostles and elders, and reported all that God had done through them. Then some of the Pharisaic party who had become believers came forward and said, "They must be circumcised and told to keep the Law of Moses."

The apostles and elders held a meeting to look into this matter; and, after a long debate, Peter rose and addressed them . . . .

At that the whole company fell silent and listened to Barnabas and Paul as they told of all the signs and miracles that God had worked among the Gentiles through them. When they had finished speaking, James summed up . . . .

"My judgement therefore is that we should impose no irksome restrictions on those of the Gentiles who are turning to God, but instruct them by letter to abstain from things polluted by contact with idols, from fornication, from anything that has been strangled, and from blood." (Acts 15:1-2, 4-7, 12-13, 19-20)

Question
What actions helped to resolve the conflict?

10.

Must Everyone Agree for a Congregation to Act?

Sometimes two separate conflicts become linked and entangled. In this case study, concerned persons try to respond to a powerful institution when it appears to be violating wise public policy. Many options are available: prayer, education, letter-writing, speeches, petitions, vigils, political action, boycotts, demonstrations, and strikes. Persons in this case study chose to participate in a demonstration and a vigil.

The focus of this study is a related conflict: how can a congregation find consensus among members with varied and strongly held views?

The corporate headquarters of the Honeywell Corporation—manufacturer of thermostats, computers, MX missile guidance systems, nuclear warheads, and cluster bombs—is located in Minneapolis, Minnesota. At least a dozen Honeywell plants are located in the greater metropolitan area. Since the late 1960s a peace coalition, known as the "Honeywell Project," has called for the Honeywell Corporation to cease manufacturing military products.

In May and June of 1981, Israel's use of Honeywell-manufactured cluster bombs in the invasion of Lebanon revived interest in the Honeywell Project. Honeywell cluster bombs had been used in the Vietnam War, where the metal fragments could be detected by radar. Subsequent bombs with plastic fragments that eluded radar were used in Lebanon primarily to terrorize civilian populations.

In June a number of concerned individuals met at St. Joseph's House, a Catholic Worker women's shelter. Four members of Faith Mennonite Church, a ninety-member congregation in Minneapolis, attended along with from twenty to thirty others. The group made plans for a quiet, weekly prayer vigil at the Honeywell headquarters. Two members of Faith, Julie and Frank, took charge of one of the vigils each month. They, together with a third person, attended monthly planning sessions of the Honeywell Project. Those attending these meetings became known as the "Core Group."

When it became public knowledge that Honeywell was the major manufacturer of cluster bombs used in the Lebanese invasion, many in the Twin Cities spoke out in protest. The Honeywell Project Core Group increased from ten to more than fifty. It included members of the Fellowship of Reconciliation, the Northern Sun Alliance, and Clergy and Laity Concerned, together with anti- nuclear activists and Christian pacifists.

The Honeywell Project staged a demonstration in February 1982 at the corporation's annual stockholders' meeting. Scheduled for the Minneapolis Institute of Arts, the stockholder's meeting was moved, within two days of the meeting, to the downtown Hilton Hotel, presumably to reduce the area available for the demonstration. The protestors asked Honeywell to cancel plans for MX production, but a stockholder's motion to abandon production of the MX was defeated by a margin of ninety-eight to two. The Project sent letters to the chairman of the Honeywell board outlining four demands:

(1) Stop production of conventional weapon development and production.

(2) Stop production of nuclear weapons systems.

(3) Convert production to peacetime purposes.

(4) Give one million dollars to victims of cluster bombs in Vietnam and Lebanon, a sum equal to Honeywell's annual contribution to the United Way in Minneapolis-St. Paul.

Attempts to meet with members of the board of Honeywell were refused. The Honeywell Project made plans for a November 4 vigil and demonstration at the Honeywell headquarters. Two Honeywell board members agreed to talk with Project representatives. The board members explained, "Honeywell does only that which the U.S. government contracts. If you oppose what it is doing, address your concerns to the government." Project representatives talked with Mayor Don Fraser and Chief of Police Anthony Bouza, explaining the group's intent to hold a peaceful demonstration with no violence toward people or property. Project representatives wrote again to the chairman of the board of Honeywell, requesting his response to the four demands.

In September, Julie and Frank, members of the Honeywell Project Core Group, spoke to their congregation at Faith Mennonite. They explained the Honeywell Project and told of the planned demonstration. They asked for counsel and for possible congregational involvement. From fifteen to twenty members of the congregation had participated in the vigils. Frank and Julie had discussed these questions in their small group at church and were encouraged by the group to report on a Sunday morning.

Frank and Julie had previously presented their questions to the Faith Mennonite Church Council. The council arranged for two congregational meetings, one a general information meeting and the other a formal meeting for a decision to be made by consensus.

From thirty to forty members attended the first meeting, in which two members of the Honeywell Project steering committee, one a Catholic sister, described the project. After the two left, the group discussed the issues and raised questions about the nature of Christian pacifism. Some thought the project was too vague. Others were reluctant to support people who might do things that they could not sanction.

During the next week several Faith members attended a meeting of the Project Core Group. They were pleased to observe the Christian convictions among the fifty in attendance. Dividing into six smaller clusters, the group reviewed concerns and steps to be taken for the November 4 demonstration. A Faith participant commented:

> Here we Mennonites had input. Our major contribution was in shaping the statement to Honeywell that expressed our hope of what Honeywell could become if it ceased to be a war industry. We also talked about symbols. Some acquainted with Berrigan-led demonstrations in the East suggested the use of blood as a symbol. Others of us viewed this as too violent. Our voice was heard. The sharing of bread emerged as the central symbol of the action.

The congregation held a second informational meeting the following Sunday night. Many expressed their thoughts and doubts. The group discussed numerous questions relating to the planned November 4 action. Five Faith members had volunteered to block the entrance to the Honeywell headquarters on November 4—two to take the action and three to lend support. At this second informational meeting the congregation was invited to respond to three proposals: (1) Make a statement of support for the five in the November 4 action, (2) make a donation to the Project for a leaflet explaining the witness, and (3) write letters of concern to congressional delegates and to the chairman of the board of Honeywell.

For the previous several weeks Sunday school classes at Faith had been working through the study guide "Justice and the Christian Witness." Congregational members found the section on decision-making and consensus-building particularly significant. Before the first congregational meeting the pastor arranged a worship service and preached a sermon focused on "Holy Obedience."

Following the two informational meetings, the congregation met on the third Sunday afternoon of October to respond to the three recommendations. This meeting drew the largest attendance on record. The congregation had agreed to act only by consensus; if anyone dissented, no decision would be made. A church member with professional experience in group process served as a resource person for the meeting. The congregation divided into small groups to review, step by step, the plans for the November 4 action and the possible congregational responses. Each person was to subscribe to one of four positions: (1) agree, (2) agree if certain modifications were made, (3) do not agree but will not stand in the way, or (4) do not agree.

Those speaking for their small groups reported support for the recommendations. However, some expressed difficulty with the wording that the two men who had volunteered to demonstrate were to be the "congregation's representatives." Some confessed they had acted little on the Honeywell issue. The congregation agreed to change the wording in the first recommendation to the following: "We support Frank and Troy with our prayers and our financial support if need be."

One participant observed, "The consensus process elevated the minority position. Everyone had to say what he or she thought." In one of the small groups two older people commented, "When this was first discussed we couldn't support the action, but after the two congregational meetings we could support it." All but one member, Jim, supported one of the first three proposals. Jim had to leave the meeting early and could not be contacted. The congregation felt that it was unfair to decide without his input.

The congregation recessed the meeting until the following Sunday afternoon. A member in Jim's small group, designated to talk with him, learned that his objection was that any act outside of the political process should first exhaust all legal and political means. Everyone seemed to agree with this, but it raised the question, "What does it mean to exhaust all possibilities?" Jim felt he was being "railroaded." He visited with the pastor and wrote a letter which members of his small group found in their mailboxes.

Some were offended and felt he was consciously subverting the process. One of the deacons, as well as five others, talked with Jim.

The recessed congregational meeting resumed the following Sunday afternoon. Jim did not attend. A member whom Jim had authorized to speak for him reported: "Jim no longer dissents. He agrees to the consensus. He does not wish to stand in the way. He has reread John Howard Yoder's book *Nevertheless*, which impressed him as to the varieties of gifts in the church." Jim was quoted further as saying, "If I must stay with the militarists of Honeywell or with the Christian pacifists, I stay with you."

The congregation came to a consensus in support of participation in the November 4 action and agreed to appropriate $100 to prepare and publish a leaflet for distribution at the action. In its statement, the congregation expressed its Christian peace concerns and its support of the November 4 demonstration but did not give blanket approval for everything which might take place. Members agreed to stand ready to raise bail money if any were arrested.

Five members of the congregation were absent from the congregational meeting because they were attending a training session at a retreat center fifty miles away. The training group and other participants in the Honeywell Project were keenly interested in the deliberations that Sunday afternoon at Faith Mennonite Church. One Honeywell Project participant reflected on the role of the congregation:

> Mennonites had an influence far beyond their numbers, particularly as to the form of the action, the use of symbols, and in the reinforcement of Christian motivation. . . . One demonstrator, a self-proclaimed agnostic, was always interested in hearing what was happening at Faith. . . . The last Core meeting was terrific. We talked about forgiveness, seeing the opponent as a child of God, preparing oneself to forgive one's opponents, and never losing sight that our methods are aimed to bring others to a change of mind and spirit.

Five members of Faith Mennonite Church were among those engaged in the direct action on November 4. Two others from Faith led a group of six hundred in singing at the rally. Many from the congregation were present for the rally, which incorporated singing, silence, and the breaking and sharing of bread. Loaves of bread were distributed. Each person received a piece from his or her neighbor and said, "This bread represents ...," filling in a word of information or witness related to the symbol of the bread or to faith convictions. The following morning thirty-six persons were arrested for blocking entrances. One was a member of the Faith Mennonite Church.

Several years after these events, the pastor reflected on the experience:

> That whole process, potentially so divisive, really seemed to bring our congregation together. Although not everyone was or is convinced that civil disobedience is proper, through that process we seemed to have developed an affirmation for another's Christian experience and witness.... I think that process of reaching consensus on such a controversial issue was a real turning point for our congregation.

Questions

1. Discuss the congregation's agreement not to act if even one person dissented. What does "consensus" mean to you?

2. Note that the Faith Mennonite participants in the protest "had an influence far beyond their numbers." Why do you think their influence was so strong?

3. Why do you think the "potentially divisive" process used by Faith Mennonite served instead to "bring our congregation together"?

4. How do members of your congregation feel about nonviolent civil disobedience? Could you design a process for your congregation to deal constructively with potentially divisive issues?

Asserting One's Authority

Jesus went up to Jerusalem. In the temple courts he found men selling cattle, sheep and doves, and others sitting at tables exchanging money. So he made a whip out of cords, and drove all from the temple area, both sheep and cattle; he scattered the coins of the money changers and overturned their tables. To those who sold doves he said, "Get these out of here! How dare you turn my Father's house into a market!" (John 2:13-16, NIV)

Question

In what was Jesus' power in dealing with wrong: his whip? his dramatic action in overturning tables? a threat of bodily injury? his commanding moral presence?

11.

Solving a Problem Through Fasting, Praying, and Listening

Every congregation has its own set of experiences, gifts, and limitations. Ways of resolving conflict need to be tailored to the uniqueness of each group. Groups can be more resourceful in trying new methods. The procedures followed for group decision-making in this case study appear to be rooted in biblical precedent.

Members of Clearview Community Church had to come thirty minutes early to be assured of a place to sit for the Sunday morning service. In 1960, forty-three charter members had established this interdenominational church in an expanding community with several prospering industries and a growing liberal arts college. People were attracted to the church because of its friendly spirit and informal worship patterns. In its earliest days the congregation met in the community room of the town library.

In 1960, shortly after members signed the charter, the congregation purchased a small church building from a local Methodist group that had moved to a larger structure. The newly purchased Clearview building seated 140 comfortably and had a full basement. Members of Clearview Community Church plunged into several weeks of intensive painting and remodeling. This created a strong sense of unity and enthusiasm. The congregation grew rapidly. Its leaders encouraged everyone to find a role in the church program. Young families were particularly attracted to Clearview. In worship services people shared their experiences of the past week and how God had been meaningful to them. Students from the college began to attend in large numbers. In ten years the congregation increased threefold, with the membership in 1970 at 121 with an additional sixty children.

Congregational members were pleased that Clearview was so popular with college students. However, many were annoyed that these "outsiders" were forcing families to find seating on chairs placed in the aisles, in a side room, in the choir loft, and in the basement, which had a public-address outlet. Increasingly, members said to one another: "Something must be done."

Some suggested having two worship services, one before Sunday school and one after. Other proposals included building a new wing, helping to start a second congregation, razing the present structure and building a new larger building at the same location, and selling the present building and constructing a new facility elsewhere. Some, predicting that student interest would level off, urged the congregation to wait.

In calling for the annual meeting the church council announced that the future of the congregation would be discussed. Two weeks before the annual meeting one member shared on a Sunday morning that he and his wife had discussed and prayed about the situation and were led of the Spirit to give five acres on the edge of town to build a new church.

Many members had conflicting feelings: appreciation to this couple who had offered a generous gift, and displeasure at being pushed to a particular answer when the congregation had not yet had opportunity to discuss all the possibilities. The annual meeting was a long one with many reports and with little time to discuss the building needs of Clearview. The congregation expressed formally their appreciation to the couple for the offer of land. Three members spoke cautiously but with intensity that they felt they were being asked to make a premature decision. Someone moved that the congregation meet again the following month to discuss congregational building needs.

At that meeting one member reported that she knew of a congregation which had devoted a week to prayer, fasting, and church planning. She said that she was ready to try prayer and fasting. She suggested that for one week members of the congregation pledge to fast in some way, to pray for guidance, and to come together each evening for an hour to discuss one of the options. Another suggested that during the evening sessions someone from the church council present one option as convincingly as possible. Further, he urged that all discussion should be positive— that is, seeking to develop each of the various options into viable alternatives. A retired pastor in the congregation urged that each day everyone read Isaiah 58 in addition to praying for guidance. The congregation voted overwhelmingly to follow the proposed method and to begin in two weeks.

The church council named the nightly series "Planning Through Fasting, Praying, and Listening." Each evening at 6:30 the congregation considered a different option and joined in a period of prayer:

Monday—remodel the present building
Tuesday—sell the present building and build a new plant
Wednesday—build a new structure in the present location
Thursday—leave the present structure as it is with minor renovations but make more effective use of the present space by offering two services
Friday—help to start a daughter congregation
Saturday—on this wrap-up evening, the congregation joined in a simple meal and shared blessings and insights received during the week

During the week, when members pointed out the weaknesses of an option, the church council president reminded them gently that they were to speak positively of the option. More often, members gave additional arguments in favor of an option. Approximately sixty persons attended each of the evening meetings and eighty-five participated in the Saturday evening supper or "love feast." The sharing period afterward drew many comments:

- Skipping breakfast and lunch made me think hard about Clearview.
- This is a good discipline; let's do it again.
- I became aware that the church is more than a building.
- I can now see three acceptable answers to our problem.
- I could feel the unity of the church grow as the week progressed.
- This was like a revival service.
- I am more puzzled than ever about what is the best move for us, but am ready to accept anything the group decides.
- Why haven't we used the method of prayer and fasting before? It helps to keep one's mind and spirit in focus.

Other congregations heard about the Clearview experience and asked whether members would recommend the method for other churches.

Questions

1. Was the couple's offer of five acres for a new church building helpful?

2. What aspects of the procedure followed by the Clearview Community Church most appeal to you?

3. Can you envision your congregation adapting this method for use in handling a complex issue?

Negotiating with God.

So the Lord said, "There is a great outcry over Sodom and Gomorrah; their sin is very grave. I must go down and see whether their deeds warrant the outcry which has reached me. I am resolved to know the truth." When the men turned and went towards Sodom, Abraham remained standing before the Lord. Abraham drew near him and said, "Wilt thou really sweep away good and bad together? Suppose there are fifty good men in the city; wilt thou sweep it away, and not pardon the place because of the fifty good men? Far be it from thee to do this—to kill good and bad together; for then the good would suffer with the bad. Far be it from thee. Shall not the judge of all the earth do what is just?"

The Lord said, "If I find in the city of Sodom fifty good men, I will pardon the whole place for their sake." Abraham replied, "May I presume to speak to the Lord, dust and ashes that I am: suppose there are five short of the fifty good men? Wilt thou destroy the whole city for a mere five men?" He said, "If I find forty-five there I will not destroy it." Abraham spoke again, "Suppose forty can be found there?" and he said, "For the sake of the forty I will not do it." Then Abraham said, "Please do not be angry, O Lord, if I speak again: suppose thirty can be found there?" He answered, "If I find thirty there I will not do it." Abraham continued, "May I presume to speak to the Lord: suppose twenty can be found there?" He replied, "For the sake of the twenty I will not destroy it." Abraham said, "I pray thee not to be angry, O Lord, if I speak just once more: suppose ten can be found there?" He said, "For the sake of the ten I will not destroy it." When the Lord had finished talking with Abraham, he left him, and Abraham returned home. (Genesis 18:20-33)

Questions
1. What were Abraham's qualities as a negotiator?
2. What were God's qualities as a negotiator?

12.

A Congregation Decides to Build

Building programs have a reputation for tearing congregations apart: many decisions, many conflicts over preference, many demands on time and money. Factions can develop over program priorities, and church leaders often bear the brunt of congregational dividedness.

This is a study of a congregation that grew stronger despite the challenges of a major building effort.

In 1972, the Hankerton Disciples of Christ Church began to discuss alternatives to its inadequate facilities. For more than forty years members had met for worship, fellowship, and Sunday school in a modest, attractive frame building on Main Street. During the past decade the growing congregation had experimented with ways of easing its space problem. Several adult and youth Sunday school classes met at private homes. On Sunday mornings latecomers found their way to the balcony and to a small windowed room at the back of the sanctuary.

Although the church board recommended to the three-hundred member congregation that it ought to experiment with two worship services, most members resisted the idea. One person summed up the views of many when she stated at a congregational meeting: "Scheduling two services will be, at best, a temporary solution to ease our problem. We are a community-oriented church which emphasizes close Christian fellowship. Let's look at long-term solutions that will build up our commitment to unity."

During the next year families of the congregation met monthly in "cell groups" to explore alternatives for meeting its space needs. The cell-group arrangement allowed for each member to offer suggestions and to voice concerns. A coordinating committee gathered information about the congregation and made a study of future growth trends. It concluded that the too-crowded facility was likely to hinder future church growth.

Although the congregation considered for a time the possibility of remodeling and enlarging its present building, the option appeared unsatisfactory to many. The Disciples of Christ building, located on a busy street corner, was hemmed in by well-established businesses. In addition, parking had long been a problem.

After two years and numerous congregational meetings, a majority of members concluded that it would be best to build at another location. A newly created building committee hired a local architect. Because the congregation had considered the facility problem for so long, lay members worked closely with the architect in designing a new building suited to the congregation's needs.

Most members supported enthusiastically the congregational decision to build at a new location. But some of the older members felt uneasy about the plan. Although they were silent at congregational meetings, this minority of members visited among themselves. As young persons and charter members of the church some forty years before, they had raised the money, planned, and carried out the building of the present structure. While they acknowledged that the church had become uncomfortably crowded, they did not feel prepared to embark on a major building program.

Persons in church leadership knew of the unhappiness of a

few of the older church members. They realized that putting the original building up for sale would be painful to charter members who had a lifetime of memories bound up with the church structure. The pastor, who was well acquainted with the elderly parishioners, was concerned that this minority group feel appreciated and become a part of the congregational process of building. He arranged for the building committee chairman, a young father, to meet with groups of older members, answering their questions and soliciting their advice. During these meetings the pastor and the building committee chairman asserted that the congregation valued the lifelong contributions of the older members. The committee chairman, realizing the importance of working with the senior members, vowed to listen to and care for each congregational member throughout the planning process.

Another minority group in the congregation was more vocal. A few members, concerned about financial stewardship, opposed the plan to build elsewhere. At a congregational meeting a young woman spoke up: "What about the needs elsewhere in the world? How can we justify spending hundreds of thousands of dollars on ourselves? Are we buying comfort while ignoring desperate needs overseas?"

Since such members were outspoken, they played a large role in the planning of the building. Although they had at first dismissed the idea of building new, they came to support the project. The building and financial planning committees instructed the architect to design an energy-efficient, multiple-use building. Stewardship concerns were often at the fore of planning discussions. As a result of these individuals' influence the church decided against purchasing a new organ.

As the date for groundbreaking approached, some congregational members asked whether much of the labor might not be donated by the members themselves. Two builders in the congregation accepted an invitation to lead the congregation in a year of voluntary service of building the church. Although the building committee contracted out some aspects of the project to specialists, church members did all of the carpentry work.

While nearly everyone involved with the project approved of the volunteer building effort, a lone member, a union mason, was unhappy with the church's unconventional labor arrangement. He argued that the church's actions were unethical in light of unemployment among some local construction trades. The two men in charge of the building project met with him to explain their perspective. But he continued to oppose the church's decision. Before the project was completed he requested a letter to transfer membership to a nearby church.

Most of the members of the congregation were unaware of this conflict. They also failed to notice or question the reasons of a few inactive members who left the congregation. In general, the congregation expressed positive feelings and experiences about its building project. When the new building was completed and the original structure sold, the congregation celebrated the fact that the older members had remained a part of the process. They did not speak of some human costs of the building project.

Some months after the project was completed, an eighty-year-old member told his children of some of the difficulties that, forty years earlier, the charter members had encountered in *their* building experience. He confided: "We overcame that struggle and succeeded in reaching our goal. At the time we thought our new building would be permanent, but we didn't realize that each new generation wants to build its own monument."

Questions

1. What are the advantages and disadvantages of handling important issues in small groups? What is the function of a "coordinating committee" in this setting?

2. Do you believe that the older members and others opposed to building were adequately involved in the decision-making process?

3. Could anything have been done to meet the concerns of the union mason who opposed the unconventional labor arrangement?

4. Is significant change generally accompanied by conflict? Can you recall situations where you or others pushed for change and in the

process damaged a relationship? Can you recall times when in order to avoid conflict you failed to pursue necessary changes?

Don't Go to Bed Angry

Then throw off falsehood; speak the truth to each other, for all of us are the parts of one body. If you are angry, do not let anger lead you into sin; do not let sunset find you still nursing it; leave no loop-hole for the devil. . . .

No bad language must pass your lips, but only what is good and helpful to the occasion, so that it brings a blessing to those who hear it. . . . Have done with spite and passion, all angry shouting and cursing, and bad feeling of every kind.

Be generous to one another, tender-hearted, forgiving one another as God in Christ forgave you. . . . (Ephesians 4:25-27, 29, 31-32)

Questions

1. How does lingering anger injure relationships?

2. When does it help and when does it injure to speak passionately, even angrily?

13.

A Storm over a Church Split

If a congregation seeks to resolve a conflict, it most often draws on its own people to handle the problem. Sometimes a congregational conflict is so intense, deeply imbedded, and polarized that members recognize the need for an experienced mediator. A mediator can bring skills, resourcefulness, and hope to deteriorating group relationships. This is a study, told in first person, of a mediator's attempt to help one congregation. Although mediators have differing styles, here is an approach that commends itself for other situations.

For several months I had been hearing about a congregation caught in a storm of disagreement. Its pastor had taken a public stand on a controversial issue and this brought an outcry from many individuals in the church who felt they could no longer support the pastor. The congregational chairman and several other leaders in the church met with conference officials to discuss the matter. In the next months church members encountered other unresolved issues but failed to deal openly with them. Hoping to reduce injury to himself and the congregation, the pastor resigned.

A few weeks after the resignation, supporters of the pastor announced that they planned to leave the congregation to start a new church. They maintained that revenge was not their purpose,

but asserted that the remainder of the congregation had given little encouragement to them in their own vision for the church.
Besides, they added, few Mennonite churches existed in the city
and it would be well to establish another congregation with a new
mission and identity. They hoped to maintain cooperative ties
with their home church.

Anger and acrimony burned within the congregation. Although the departing group had expressed a desire for cooperation, many within it were angry about what they felt were unfair
charges against the resigned pastor. Members of the remaining
group felt falsely accused and deeply pained by the departure of
the others, some of whom were gifted leaders.

I received a call from the congregational chairman who six
months earlier had participated in a regional Mennonite Conciliation Service seminar on congregational conflict. If the church
chose to invite a mediator to assist them, would I consider coming? We discussed expectations of such an intervention, costs,
dates, and how the chairman should carry this possibility back to
the church. He decided to discuss the matter with the church
elders. If they approved, he would recommend to the church the
use of an outside mediator at a forthcoming congregational meeting.

Several weeks later he was back on the phone again, report-
ing the congregation's decision to invite me. Since the situation
had been deteriorating for many months, we decided to schedule
the intervention as soon as possible, on a Wednesday and Thursday evening three weeks hence. I asked him to arrange for several
individuals representing opposing views to phone me.

I voiced my key concern to the church chairman: What did
he believe we might accomplish from this intervention? He
responded that church members needed to be able to talk together constructively about what had been happening, about why
one group was leaving—reasons which remained confusing to the
remaining group—and about what would happen next within the
congregation. He agreed that the main goal must be open com-

munication rather than reuniting the congregation. Although our time together would be short, I felt confident we could enter into significant dialogue in two evenings.

As I had requested, two individuals with differing viewpoints phoned me. My usual approach in these conversations is to ask first for a brief description of what is happening. I follow this with an inquiry about my coming to the group—do most people feel supportive? Sometimes one side perceives the presence of an outsider as a manipulative move by the other side. I want to be aware of such sentiment early so that I can contact persons suspicious of my involvement. My third question relates to goals: What do you personally hope we can accomplish? Sometimes the goals of various groups differ substantially, requiring further discussion within the church, a conference phone call with the mediator, and careful attention to goal clarification. Our conversations revealed no such discrepancies and I was satisfied that the church was prepared for intervention. I asked the church chairman to appoint a small council representing the range of viewpoints.

After arriving at the church, I met for two hours with this council. First I focused on learning to know individuals and their roles in the church. Then I asked them what they believed was causing the current situation and what they hoped we could accomplish during the next few evenings. Finally, I asked whether it was likely that the people most important to the success of this dialogue would be present. Sometimes leaders in the church stay home out of resentment or weariness. A phone call or two of encouragement, especially from those who have already met the mediator and can report that he or she seems to be a principled and gentle person, can bring in important foot-draggers.

Evening arrived. As always in the first meeting, the group straggling into the church basement was subdued and tense. Nevertheless, I felt surprise that church members appeared normal and friendly, a never-failing response on my part to first encounters with a group about which I've been hearing tales of woe for many weeks.

I began with a biblical meditation on 1 Thessalonians 5:21, "Despise not prophecy, but test everything," emphasizing the importance of persons taking a stand but also of testing all perspectives critically. This requires dialogue and disagreement, so it is healthy for groups to hear what others have to say and to submit their own views to critical scrutiny.

In order to ensure that everyone had realistic and similar expectations for our time together, I led a brief goal clarification exercise. First I stated that I would like the help of about ten people in an informal discussion about what we hoped to accomplish during the two meetings. Arbitrarily I identified persons from several rows and asked if they were willing to participate in an off-the-cuff discussion. We pulled chairs into a circle for this group and I added one additional empty chair. Anyone wishing to add anything to the discussion could come and join the conversation for several minutes. I requested that we go around the circle, each person stating what he or she hoped we might accomplish. I took notes for everyone to see on newsprint and identified the goals on which I felt we could make progress as well as ones which would require long-term efforts.

Because time was limited, we had no option but to move rapidly to the heart of the disagreement. I wanted to arrange for open dialogue in a way that involved as many people as possible. I announced that a major issue in the congregation had been the stated intention of one group to start a new fellowship, and that I wanted to guide a discussion of this issue and what lay behind it. I designated one end of the room to represent those who definitely intended to leave the congregation, and the other end, those who definitely intended to stay. Between these two points was an area which represented a wide range of intermediate views. After a minute, I asked everyone to walk to a point on the spectrum that represented their views. The group gave a collective gulp at the prospect of revealing publicly their intentions. Then, chuckling nervously, they found their places.

Having chosen a position, people were unsure what to do.

Was it legitimate to peek? Like many churches, this group believed it was wrong or at least risky to publicly expose disagreement. I assured them that peeking was allowed, indeed, encouraged. Then I invited people to share aloud why they stood where they did. Responses came readily and thoughtfully from all around the room.

Next I formed three groups: one from each of the ends of the spectrum and a third from those in the middle. I directed the two polar groups to list their responses to the questions "How do we perceive the other polar group?" and "How do we think they perceive us?" I directed the middle group to prepare a list describing perceptions of both sides and the dilemmas of being "in the middle." After thirty minutes I asked a reporter from each group to share the lists aloud. It was a sobering experience.

We were due for a break. We had not had time to discuss these lists together as a group and I was concerned that personal conversations might begin during the break that would grow hostile. So I requested silence; all greetings and communication during the break were to be nonverbal. The result surprised me. As persons walked past each other, they nodded, shook hands, and embraced, often with tears in their eyes. The rule of silence enabled them to set aside their rational differences and experience the powerful emotional desire for understanding and comfort.

Although I was touched and encouraged by these gestures, I was also concerned that the timing of this experience was out of sync with other tasks. We had not explored in depth the very real differences within the group and I knew that painful as it would be, we could not bypass them. I would have preferred for these moments of embrace to have come *after* we had openly discussed critical differences. This would have helped to mark a definite turn toward restored relationships. I feared that returning to the unresolved issues would take us in the wrong direction. In vain I searched for some way to carry further the gestures of reconciliation, then decided to view them as encouraging statements of commitment despite unresolved differences. After the break we continued as I had planned.

I asked the two polar groups to prepare a list of "things which block us from reconciliation." After twenty minutes I asked them to read these lists aloud. The lists were long and complex. I could feel a sense of hopelessness settle over the group as we finished.

This concluded our exercises for the first evening. I felt uncomfortable about ending our first session on this note. The problems seemed overwhelming and we had made no tangible progress. I feared that no one would want to return for the second evening. Since the hour was late I dismissed the group, acknowledging that we had heard many weighty problems, yet had made a significant step by bringing these problems to the surface. Tomorrow night, I reminded them, we would move forward from this emotional low point of our discussion and begin clarifying events and perceptions.

The next evening at seven o'clock I began with an exercise of affirmation. Continuing with the existing groups, I gave each one an opportunity to state appreciation or gratitude about individuals in the other groups. In heartwarming response, individuals offered affirmations in all directions.

Now we moved to the core of the problem. Both polar groups worked separately with their lists of concerns which blocked them from reconciliation. In a few minutes they condensed and prioritized the lists. Members of the middle group moved their chairs to the sides of the room and the polar groups faced each other. Then I asked a reporter from one group to read the first item on the list, and for those in that same group for whom this was of significant concern to raise their hands. I then asked for several individual comments from those raising their hands. Why was this issue significant? How had it affected them personally? I wanted to connect the issue in a concrete way to persons and emotions. After several individuals had spoken, I turned to the other polar group and asked if anyone could respond helpfully to the item raised. Responses came readily, leading to further comments by the first group.

By 8:45 we had covered much ground and the atmosphere was improving steadily. But we had only gotten to the first item on each group's list, and in both groups there remained five or six additional items. I had emphasized from the beginning that we would not have time to cover nearly all the items of disagreement about the past. Aware that we had several crucial steps yet to take beyond airing perceptions about the past, I felt we must move on, and decided to risk doing so. If it became apparent that specific topics blocked the discussion, we could return to them later if necessary.

The middle group had not yet addressed the polar groups but was impatient to do so. The middle group was twice the size of either polar group and held potential as a powerful mediating force. We now turned to these persons for insight. They were critical of both polar groups, frustrated that both had listened poorly. Both had jumped to early conclusions. The middle group suggested further dialogue betweeen the two poles and voiced their desire to be a mediating force.

We began a new discussion by listing options for the future: staying together as a church with ongoing conversations about key differences; separating into two independent churches; separating but exploring ways of cooperation and mutual support. Most agreed that the first option was unrealistic. Members of one group had already met several times and were enthusiastic about beginning a new church in the city. The second option was unattractive, for only a few wished to relinquish all ties with their old fellowship. But many nodded affirmatively when someone suggested the third option of mutual support.

We had made important progress but a crucial additional step remained. We needed to agree on some structure responsible to carry forward this intention. Who would lead the congregation in the stage of cooperative planning? It was after ten o'clock and a major further discussion was not possible. Although as a facilitator I prefer to have the group generate ideas, I offered an idea of my own. What about having each of the two poles identify one or two people responsible for selecting several additional representatives for the proposed discussions? Both poles liked the idea. "But what about us?" queried persons in the middle group. "We have valid concerns about both sides," commented one. Someone suggested that the middle group be represented in negotiations as well. This enabled the group to do what it had been eager to do all along, to serve in the much needed role of mediator. A straw vote demonstrated strong support for this structure.

Despite the lateness of the hour, we spent an additional ten minutes in one last step toward reconciliation. Before taking my seat, I invited the congregational members to offer statements of appreciation, statements of intent to cooperate with or support further efforts of understanding, and statements of apology or regret about earlier actions. Individuals rose one after another and offered statements of reconciliation. My heart filled with gratitude. The hurt and pain of many months of misunderstanding was beginning to find healing in these minutes. Not every intervention reaches this point of open confession, and I knew that having reached this moment, the likelihood of restoring respect among these diverse individuals was high. Often I have asked two reconciling parties to sign a statement at this point in the intervention process, but I sensed that in this setting a written statement was unnecessary.

One month later I returned for the first meeting of the nine members of the "negotiating group." We identified a list of issues needing resolution. Then we formed three small working groups, each comprised of representatives from the three spectrum groups. Each working group spent forty minutes listing all possible options for two separate issues and then reported to the gathered negotiating group. When issues seemed especially significant or volatile, I led the entire negotiating group in discussion, listing the "pluses and minuses" of each option.

After the initial meeting, the negotiating group continued to meet and to move forward with only phone assistance on my part.

Over the course of several meetings, combined with regular report and consultation with the two active churches, the negotiating group was able to agree on steps for ongoing cooperation.

Questions
1. List step by step the actions of the mediator which appear to have helped resolve the conflict. In what ways could he have increased his effectiveness?

2. Can you name any "new churches" begun by groups that splintered away from established churches? Identify situations in which it would be better to flee than fight.

3. What are the advantages and disadvantages of inviting an outside party (such as a trained mediator) to help resolve a conflict?.

Agreeing to Disagree

After a while Paul said to Barnabas, "Ought we not to go back now to see how our brothers are faring in the various towns where we proclaimed the word of the Lord?" Barnabas wanted to take John Mark with them; but Paul judged that the man who had deserted them in Pamphylia and had not gone on to share in their work was not the man to take with them now. The dispute was so sharp that they parted company. Barnabas took Mark with him and sailed for Cyprus, while Paul chose Silas. He started on his journey, commended by the brothers to the grace of the Lord. (Acts 15:36-40)

Question
Sometimes people can't agree. What alternatives might have been considered for the resolution of this conflict?

14.
The Dismissal of the Pastor for Want of One Vote

Many congregational constitutions require a two-thirds ma-jority of members present and voting both to call and to reappoint a pastor. This assures the pastor of strong support. This two-thirds requirement is a convenient rule for decision-making, but some-times it presents difficulties during reappointment or termination. Many congregational controversies center on the hiring and firing of a pastor. Are there lessons to be learned on how to appoint, reappoint, and dismiss a pastor wisely and sensitively? Following are stories from four congregations:

Congregation A—recognized as a strong, rural, traditional, conference-supportive congregation with a history of able min-isters—called, during the late sixties, a new pastor by unanimous vote. He had served three congregations and his appointment had been renewed each term. He was an aggressive, friendly person who supported conference programs, urged increased giving for church causes and was active in community affairs. He was criticized for defending a young high school football coach at the end of his first losing season when many irate fans were calling that the coach be fired. Although many appreciated the pastor's sermons, some felt that they were too long. A few members were offended that his youngest son, a conscientious objector, refused to register for the draft during the Vietnam War. Some were even more disturbed that his daughter, active in the student protest movement, no longer attended church when she returned from college. An older member commented: "A lot of changes are taking place in our community; we are not as unified as we once thought we were."

A day or two before the annual meeting, when the question of the reappointment of the pastor was to be on the agenda, several members who were displeased with the pastor phoned a number of less active members and urged them to attend the meeting to vote on the pastor. When they phoned, they said, "The church is falling apart because of all the dissatisfaction with the pastor." One hundred persons attended the annual meeting, twenty to thirty more than usual. On the vote to reappoint the pastor for a second three-year term, sixty-six voted for and thirty-four against, a fraction less than the two-thirds required. The pastor and his wife were devastated. They had not anticipated such a negative vote. Many of the supporters of the pastor were angry that inactive members had been called in to reject the pastor. Bitter feelings permeated the congregational membership.

Congregation B, located in a prosperous small town, was served by a pastor who was well liked by young people but whom some considered too informal and lighthearted. He preached sermons which held the attention of the congregation but were often too off-beat for the tastes of many. He was criticized for his irregularity in visiting older members. After five years as pastor he received an invitation to become pastor of a church in another state. He asked the board of deacons, all good friends with whom he worked closely, whether he should consider seriously this invitation. The deacons acknowledged that there was some dissatisfaction which he could dispel; they encouraged him to stay. He declined the invitation which he had been tempted to accept. Six months later, at the congregational meeting to decide future leadership, he failed to receive the approval of two-thirds. The vote at this poorly attended meeting was forty-one for and twenty-two against. He could not suppress feelings of bitterness toward the deacons, whom he had asked for advice a few months earlier. Soon he would be without a job and he felt unprepared for this crisis.

Congregation C, one of the larger and older congregations in the conference, had the same pastor for thirty years and then had a series of pastors, each of whom stayed only a few years. The congregation had several strong groups. The original core group of successful farm families and business and professional people were among the most respected in the community. A growing group included young couples, many of whom worked in a nearby city and were attracted to this well-established church. Most of these couples were unfamiliar with the spiritual heritage of the conference with its emphases on peace, missions, and service. A third group was highly critical of the conference affiliation. Some of these urged that the congregation become an independent Bible church and develop close relations with students from a nearby Bible institute.

A young pastor, who with his wife had attended a fundamentalist Bible institute and a church college, was recommended to the congregation as having gifts which would appeal to all three groups. Both the pastor and his wife had deep interest and thorough seminary preparation in biblical studies. This was the pastor's second church assignment, and he was not fully skilled in all the pastoral arts. During Wednesday evening Bible studies, which he and his wife taught jointly, he was criticized for not using certain terms and phrases and for failing to emphasize certain doctrines. At the congregational meeting to decide on his reappointment, he received seventy-three votes to forty-one opposed, just short of two-thirds. The pastor and his wife were not surprised by the rejection but they were disappointed. They had hoped that through a strong Bible study program they could bring the congregation together.

Congregation D, a growing congregation in a small city, had two painful experiences with the two-thirds rule. Two former pastors had served only one term because they lacked a few votes of the necessary two-thirds. Distressed by these events, the congregation changed the constitution to provide for election and reappointment of the pastor by simple majority vote. The action also called for an annual evaluation of the pastor by the board of deacons. The deacons used an outline of questions to guide the evaluation. The annual evaluation was a two to three-hour session with the pastor's wife and youth pastor present. Everyone was encouraged to contribute criticisms, concerns, satisfactions and hopes.

A growing number of members felt it was time for the pastor, who had served nine years, to take another pastorate. These concerns were stated cautiously in the evaluation sessions. At the annual meeting the pastor received 55 percent of the vote of those present, the remaining 45 percent divided betweeen "no" votes and abstentions. Later, the pastor told his conference minister that he was pleased with the support he had received from the deacons in the evaluation session and that he had concluded that the congregational abstentions were more or less supportive. The chairperson of the board of deacons told the conference minister that the deacons had reported to the pastor more dissatisfaction than he had acknowledged and that they had really encouraged him to look for another position.

The pastor remained despite mounting opposition that was not openly expressed. At the next congregational meeting a member moved that the constitution be changed to restore the two-thirds rule for pastoral elections and reappointments. In presenting his motion he declared: "The two-thirds rule is a good American tradition." Another responded that she knew of no biblical examples of settling questions of leadership by majority or two-thirds vote. She said, "The biblical method should be one of consensus where we talk and pray about it until we have a meeting of minds." Another moved that the motion be amended to provide for a two-thirds vote to call a pastor and for a simple majority vote every three years for reappointment. Decision on the amendment and the motion was postponed until the next congregational meeting. Members continued to discuss appropriate ways of calling a pastor and how to terminate in an honest, loving way a pastor's service.

Questions

1. Why do many congregational controversies center on the hiring or release of a pastor?

2. What lessons can be learned from the experiences of the four congregations? What are the advantages and disadvantages of various methods (majority vote, two-thirds vote, and consensus) for deciding pastoral terms?

3. Discuss the current method used for deciding pastoral term in your congregation. How could the process be improved?

Demanding the Highest Rank

Then a jealous dispute broke out: who among them should rank highest? But he said, "In the world, kings lord it over their subjects; and those in authority are called their country's 'Benefactors.' Not so with you: on the contrary, the highest among you must bear himself like the youngest, the chief of you like a servant. For who is greater—the one who sits at table or the servant who waits on him? Surely the one who sits at table. Yet here am I among you like a servant." (Luke 22:24-27)

Question

If you and others know that you are the best, why not take the honored position? What does this have to do with conflict resolution?

15.
The Youth and Deacons at Odds

Conflicts in congregations arise from many roots: young versus old, rural versus urban, longtime member versus new arrival, innovative versus traditional, conservative versus progressive, working class versus professional. Many congregations embrace people of diverse talents and personalities. But variety can create problems.

At first glance, one may conclude that this study involves generational and theological conflicts. But one also finds other factors, such as patterns of decision-making and communication. As a result of this experience, each group learned lessons that might be applied to similar situations in the future.

The youth group of Crossroads Church raised funds to purchase copies of the Herald Press hymnal *Sing and Rejoice!* for the congregation to use along with *The Mennonite Hymnal.* More than a year after the congregation began using the new books, someone protested to the board of deacons that hymn number 67 in *Sing and Rejoice!* "Lord of the Dance," was inappropriate. They requested that something be done about it.

After a discussion, the board of deacons agreed. The board gave the youth group three choices: cut out the pages of the offending hymn from each *Sing and Rejoice!* hymnal, paste the two pages of hymn 67 together, or withdraw all copies of the hymnal from congregational use.

When members of the congregation heard of this action, many voiced disapproval of the deacons' decision. One of the adult Sunday school classes discussed the action and agreed among themselves that each would talk to one or more of the deacons. Following this intervention, the board of deacons withdrew its request. Some months passed. In one of his sermons, the pastor mentioned that there are many scriptural references to praising the Lord with dance, as, for example: "Let them praise his name in the dance: let them sing praises unto him with the timbrel and harp" (Psalm 149;3, KJV).

One Sunday, just before Christmas, members turned to the *Sing and Rejoice!* hymnal and found the following message stamped on the page of hymn 67: "We consider this song to be unworthy of our Lord. Board of Deacons." A second hymn also bore this stamp. A few weeks later at the annual congregational meeting an older member, who had once been a deacon, spoke disapprovingly of the action of the board. He cited biblical references to singing, clapping, shouting, and dancing to express joy and praise. He also questioned whether the board of deacons had exceeded its authority in acting as it did. An extended discussion followed. One of the deacons explained that the hymn was offensive not so much because of the mention of dancing but because of its joyfulness. He observed that as one reads the biblical account of Christ's passion and crucifixion, one finds a story of sadness and sorrow. Others spoke in support of the deacons: "These are men of God whom we have elected. It is not for us to question what they have been led to do for the good of the congregation."

Three of the deacons chose not to allow their names to be considered for reelection. New deacons were elected at the annual meeting. Members of the youth group, together with supporters, were distressed with the way the deacons had handled the issue. Some wondered whether the question should be raised again with the board of deacons, now that it contained some new members.

Some felt that they should not put the new deacons in the position of having to second-guess their predecessors but should, rather, allow the issue to rest for a time. Some pointed out that, after all, the congregation still had and could use the hymnals which the youth had given.

Within two years, the Crossroads congregation adopted a statement which affirmed the *Sing and Rejoice!* hymnal and explained some of the biblical context of the two hymns. While the congregational statement asserted that all of the hymnal's songs "are intended for use by Christians," it also suggested that "in the interest of Christian unity" worship leaders should respect the views of the congregational members who believed particular songs to be "unworthy." The congregation agreed to insert the printed statement on the inside of its *Sing and Rejoice!* books.

Questions

1. Why do you think many members of the Crossroads Church disagreed with the board of deacons' inital demands to the youth?

2. Discuss the board of deacons' action in stamping the offending song with a message expressing disapproval. What other alternatives might have been found for the deacons and others to express deeply held feelings?

3. Role play the conflict, using the following characters: two young people, two deacons, the pastor, an older member, and two newly elected deacons.

Confronting One's Brother or Sister

But when Cephas came to Antioch, I opposed him to his face, because he was clearly in the wrong. For until certain persons came from James he was taking his meals with gentile Christians; but when they came he drew back and began to hold aloof, because he was afraid of the advocates of circumcision. The other Jewish Christians showed the same lack of principle; even Barnabas was carried away and played false like the rest. But when I saw that their conduct did not square with the truth of the Gospel, I said to Cephas, before the whole congregation, "If you, a Jew born and bred, live like a Gentile, and not like a Jew, how can you insist that Gentiles must live like Jews?" (Galatians 2:11-14)

Question

If Paul had followed the three steps of Matthew 18, as perhaps he did, how would this passage read?

16.

That Our Flag Was Still There: The Flag in the Church

And this be our motto: "in God is our trust!"
And the star-spangled banner in triumph shall wave
O'er the land of the free and the home of the brave!

Visitors from abroad often express surprise to see the United States flag displayed everywhere: not just on public buildings but also placed in front of private residences. The flag appears in beer commercials and is worn as a lapel pin, saluted at football games with the singing of "The Star-Spangled Banner," and faced as children in the classroom and men in service clubs recite the Pledge of Allegiance. The stars and stripes are also displayed behind the altar or pulpit in most church sanctuaries in the United States.

The flag entered American churches in periods of great military fervor: during the Spanish American War, World War I, World War II, and the Vietnam War. The flag crept more tardily into historic peace churches—Brethren, Friends, and Mennonites. Flags were introduced into some General Conference Mennonite churches during World War I and into more during World War

II. In most Mennonite Brethren Churches the U.S. flag is displayed. In Mennonite Church (MC) congregations and in more conservative Mennonite congregations the flag is not displayed.

The extensive exposure of the national flag is unique to the United States. In neither Canadian Mennonite churches nor other denominations is the Canadian flag placed in the church sanctuary. The national flag is not normally present where Christians worship in Europe, Asia, Africa, or South America. In the United States most Americans appear to believe that the cross and the flag belong together. In the rest of the world most Christians assume that a national flag is not appropriate to a place of worship.

The placing of the flag in the worship area is a bitterly contested issue in some Mennonite congregations. Following are three conflicts over the flag in Mennonite settings.

a. Heritage College

During the Vietnam War groups of students on a Mennonite campus spoke out and demonstrated their opposition to the war effort of the U.S. government. These public outbursts of opposition embarrassed the administration and the board of directors.

A new basketball coach, who was not well acquainted with the college's peace tradition, noted that games played on other campuses always began with the singing of the national anthem while facing the U.S. flag. Intending to contribute to school spirit, he arranged to install a flag in the gym for the first home game and arranged with the pep band to precede the game with "The Star-Spangled Banner." This action without consultation evoked an immediate burst of protest from many students and faculty.

The president, supported by the board of directors, agreed that removing the flag would cause public relations problems. He answered the criticisms of a student group by saying: "Isn't it the task of peaceful Christians not to offend the public? Does having the flag really cause harm?"

The criticism persisted. Some weeks later, after consulting with the board of directors, the president arranged to place alongside the flag a banner with the Mennonite Central Committee symbol of the dove and the cross. Rumblings continued but gradually the conflict died down.

b. *Hope Mennonite Church*

Hope Mennonite Church hosted a missionary conference with many guests. At the front of the sanctuary were both a U.S. flag and a Christian flag. One of the missionaries planning the conference came to the pastor and suggested that the flags be removed for the conference, since Christians from other lands do not display their national flags in worship areas. He said, "We do not want to offend our guests with what looks like American nationalism and the mixing of politics and religion." The pastor responded that he had never been offended by the presence of the flags, but added: "I don't know what to say. I guess it's your conference." The missionary removed the flags.

Some members of the congregation spoke appreciatively to the pastor regarding the removal of the flag, saying that they had long been bothered by this symbol of "national worship" in the sanctuary. They knew that the flag had been placed in the church by the Sunday school superintendent on the first anniversary of Pearl Harbor. He had been drafted early in the war but had been released because of a physical ailment. He had acted alone. Then during wartime no one had wanted to stir up a controversy in a community riding the crest of wartime patriotism. Except for an occasional wedding and funeral where families had arranged for temporary removal of the flag, the issue lay dormant until the missionary conference fifteen years later.

Soon after the missionary conference a young adult Sunday school class studying the biblical basis of peacemaking discussed the flag issue. With only a few exceptions, members of the class felt that the flag should be removed. They asked the pastor what could be done. He counseled against "stirring up a hornet's nest."

They persisted. They encouraged an older deacon to call for a study of the flag issue. He told them: "I have been troubled all these years when I sit with God's people in God's house and see the flag in front of us. Wouldn't it be better if we returned to the ways before the war?" At a congregational meeting, church members approved the appointment of a study committee to report at the next meeting.

The committee consisted of the older deacon, the former Sunday school superintendent who had given the flag to the church, the president of the youth group, and a young high school teacher who had joined the church three years earlier. The committee worked diligently, assigning one to study the history of the flag in Christian churches, another to inquire into the practice of other churches, and a third to write to church leaders for counsel. All studied Old and New Testament passages. The former superintendent felt he was outnumbered. Uncomfortable with the rest of the committee, he withdrew.

After six months the committee submitted its report to the congregation. The report affirmed the congregation's gratitude to a country that bestowed the blessings of freedom and democracy, and acknowledged loyalty to government as admonished by Scripture. The report reviewed the peace heritage of the church and other findings. It concluded with a statement of support for the pastor's decision to remove the flags on the occasion of the missions conference and recommended that the congregation, in keeping with its biblical traditions, not have a national flag displayed in the worship area.

The pastor was the first to speak: "I should clarify that I did not remove the flag. I presume it was done by those responsible for the conference." The former superintendent read a dissenting report. He spoke with deep feeling of his brother's death in the war while defending the freedoms of the nation. He declared that the United States, "founded on Christian principles and by Christian leaders, has been especially blessed. The flag before us reminds us never to cease praying thankfully for a country which trusts in God." A retired pastor stated: "This is too trivial an issue to take up this much congregational time. Let's get on with the task to which we are all called, preaching the gospel." A deacon responded, "I believe this is not a trivial issue. When the Roman emperor ordered the Christian to go along and put a pinch of incense on the pagan altar, the Christian said, 'This is not a trivial matter. I place God above emperor.'" After a long and occasionally angry discussion, a ballot vote was taken. The committee's recommendation was defeated 55-50.

In a few weeks someone again installed the flags at the front of the sanctuary. The committee members, who had worked conscientiously, felt let down by the congregation and the pastor. They wondered what they should have done differently. The youth expressed bitterness and spoke of starting a new congregation. The older deacon responded: "I sympathize with you, but this is neither the first nor last problem for this congregation. I will just stick in there, hoping and praying for another opportunity to take a fresh look at this issue."

Holding Firm

Next, fourteen years later, I went again to Jerusalem with Barnabas, taking Titus with us. I went up because it had been revealed by God that I should do so. I laid before them—but at a private interview with the men of repute—the gospel which I am accustomed to preach to the Gentiles, to make sure that the race I had run, and was running, should not be run in vain. Yet even my companion Titus, Greek though he is, was not compelled to be circumcised. That course was urged only as a concession to certain sham-Christians, interlopers who had stolen in to spy upon the liberty we enjoy in the fellowship of Christ Jesus. These men wanted to bring us into bondage, but not for one moment did I yield to their dictation; I was determined that the full truth of the Gospel should be maintained for you. (Galatians 2:1-5)

Question
Does the Bible give guidelines on when to hold firm and when to yield?

c. *Emmanuel Mennonite Church*

"This church experienced a painful church split way back at its beginning. No one wants to talk about it." So commented the pastor of Emmanuel Mennonite Church. "The congregation has a long history of conflict avoidance. If 10 percent say 'No,' it stops the congregation cold."

During World War II three-fourths of the drafted young men of Emmanuel entered regular military service. One fourth chose alternative service for conscientious objectors. During the war and afterward the congregation had a series of able pastors who held strong peace convictions. However, some issues they chose not to confront. One was the flag issue.

In 1944, at the time of the Normandy invasion, a group of mothers whose sons were with the American forces in Europe bought a U.S. flag and a Christian flag and placed them on the stage behind the pulpit. The women explained, "This is the least we can do to show our love for our country and our boys in the service." The pastor was not pleased that this group had acted without consultation, but he knew the anxieties they had for their sons and saw it as a temporary wartime gesture. But the flags remained after the war.

As the years passed a new generation of church members became concerned about the historic peacemaking task of the church. During the Vietnam War more of the young men chose conscientious-objector status than entered the military. At annual congregational meetings young adults asked, "Isn't it time for us to remove the flag, recognizing the American principle of separation of church and state and also recognizing that as Christians our first obedience is to Christ?" In these discussions a few opposed and a few supported the call to remove the flags. Many of the silent majority went to persons advocating flag removal and said, "I want you to know that I agree it would be better to remove the flags." The advocates of flag removal responded: "Why didn't you speak up? People respect your views." To this they said, "I'm afraid we may lose some members if we press too hard on this."

Other issues came to the fore and the flag issue slipped into the background. The congregation was seeking a new pastor. Highly recommended to them was a man who had decided to enter the ministry at the age of fifty after a successful career as a high school principal. When he came to preach a trial sermon and to meet the congregation he learned about the flag issue. The pastoral search committee was pleased with him and informed him that the committee was ready to present his name unanimously to the congregation. He responded, "I am ready to come for a two-year period, since this is my first pastorate, but I want you to decide the flag issue one way or the other before you consider me for a second term. I don't want to make a major issue of it, but for the spiritual health of the congregation this issue ought to be decided. I personally have discomfort with a flag in the place of worship and I want to be free to express my convictions." The committee agreed and the congregation extended a unanimous call, knowing that the new pastor wanted a decision made on the flag.

The pastor suggested that the church council invite an experienced mediator to provide professional services. The mediator came for a series of meetings in which there was good attendance and participation. It became clear that a growing number of members were convinced that it would be best to remove the U.S. flag. On the opposite side were a dozen or more persons, including several members of long standing who opposed removal of the flag. Those in the middle leaned toward removal but wanted to preserve the unity of the congregation. The mediator encouraged people to voice their feelings. The congregation seemed to enjoy a brainstorming session in which persons were invited to think of compromise positions which might be acceptable. Despite these efforts at mediation, the congregation could agree only to decide the issue later. Although everyone seemed to like the pastor, he held to his stipulation and announced that he would leave after two years.

A new pastor came to Emmanuel who at first did not have strong convictions on the flag issue but soon decided that it ought to be resolved. He saw the need for a strong biblical teaching ministry focused on issues of church and state, discipleship, and reconciliation. Under his leadership, many members began attending midweek Bible sessions. He and the church council decided that it was time to propose a middle ground acceptable to most congregational members. A year and a half after his arrival the following statement appeared in the monthly "Pastoral Letter":

> A month ago the church council proposed that the U.S. flag and the Christian flag be placed in the entranceway on the wall outside the library. On the wall beside the flags would be mounted a statement expressing the congregation's convictions on Christian citizenship, the flag, and the state. The council is calling a special congregational meeting for Sunday evening, April 1, at 7:00 p.m. to respond to this proposal. The council recommends that a two thirds vote of those present and voting be required for passage and that the vote be taken by ballot. The council commends for prayerful consideration this proposal to bring the congregation together on a difficult issue. We propose the following as a tentative draft of the flag statement: . . . .

Three weeks later the largest number of members in anyone's memory assembled for the congregational meeting. Members knew the arguments that would be offered on each side. Most persons were expectant yet apprehensive as to whether the issue of the flag could be resolved.

Questions

1. Is the retired pastor correct in his statement that the flag issue is trivial? How does one determine what are trivial and what are major issues?

2. Did the college board and president offer a satisfactory resolution of the flag question?

3. Evaluate step by step the conflict resolution process at Hope Mennonite Church. What steps were to be commended?

4. Evaluate the steps in the conflict resolution process at Emmanuel Mennonite Church. What steps were to be commended?

If a Man Should Do Something Wrong

We must not be conceited, challenging one another to rivalry, jealous of one another. If a man should do something wrong, my brothers, on a sudden impulse, you who are endowed with the Spirit must set him right again very gently. Look to yourself, each one of you: you may be tempted too. Help one another to carry these heavy loads, and in this way you will fulfil the law of Christ. (Galatians 5:26; 6:1-2)

Question
How should one correct a wrongdoer very gently?

School and Community

17.
How to Make Pruning Hooks out of Spears

This skit is subtitled "How to Succeed in Squelching a Great Idea with Really Too Much Trying." All of us have attended meetings where well-intentioned persons made nit-picking points or offered a variety of confusing comments. This scenario for a mini-drama is based on the passage from Isaiah 2:4. It should provoke discussion on the art of conducting a public meeting.

Minutes of the meeting of the Hebrew Committee on Relations with Other Nations, January 6, 800 B.C

Chairman: Our principal business today is consideration of a draft statement on war and peace by Mr. Isaiah. Since the statement was delivered to you by runners in advance of this meeting, let us assume that all of us have read it. If there is no objection, we will first have comments on the statement as a whole and then consider it word by word. Are there general comments?

Mr. Benjamin: The statement is too long. The olive growers in our synagogue won't even look at a statement as long as this.

Mr. Judah: In the first paragraph, where it says: "They shall beat their spears into pruning hooks and their swords into plowshares," what about slingshots, shouldn't they be included?

Chairman: How would you word the addition?

Mr. Judah: Well, the slingshots could be made into children's toys.

Chairman: Will the secretary read what he has down on that?

Secretary: "They shall beat their spears into pruning hooks and their swords into plowshares, and the slingshots shall be given to children to play with."

Mr. Jonathan: Third paragraph, line two: "Nations shall not, etc." Are we in a position to make such a positive statement? Making the final decisions is not the function of this committee.

Mr. Jehu: I agree. I suggest the following reading: "In our opinion, nation should not lift up sword against nation nor study war anymore."

Chairman: All in favor of this change say aye.

Mr. Samuels: Before we vote on that, I feel the lack in this statement of any motivation. Who are we? And why are we saying anything at all on this subject? I don't know quite how to word it, but there ought to be something about our basic Hebrew motives and objectives.

Chairman: I see Mr. Judah has been busy writing. Do you have a wording for this addition?

Mr. Judah: How about this? "As Hebrews and guardians of the law given at Sinai, it is our opinion, etc."

Mr. Jonathan: That sounds presumptuous. We are not the only Hebrews and guardians of the law. We have no right to speak for everybody.

Mr. Judah: You are probably right. How about this? "As the Committee on Relations with Other Nations and as .001 percent of the guardians of the law and speaking only for ourselves, we are on the whole of the opinion, etc."

Mr. Benjamin: I'm not quite satisfied with the reference to pruning hooks. Let's be realistic. If all the spears in the country were turned into pruning hooks, we'd have more pruning hooks than we'd know what to do with.

Mr. Jehu: Mr. Chairman, I move that a subcommittee be appointed to redraft Mr. Isaiah's statement, taking into account the suggestions made here, and that we meet again after the new moon to consider the revision.

Mr. Eliphaz: I hope the subcommittee will take into consideration that the comma in the third line from the top ought to be a semicolon.

Chairman: Thank you very much, gentlemen. I think we all want to thank Mr. Isaiah for his very fine statement. At our next meeting I hope we can come up with something really good.

Questions

1. Recall experiences from your past that this skit brings to mind. How can people of goodwill become a part of the problem in decision-making?

2. What could the chairperson have done to better manage the meeting?

3. Can you identify some situations in which it is appropriate to use a consensus process to make decisions, and others in which one person needs to decide?

18.
Students Challenge Their Instructor

In many relationships one person holds power over another: coach over player, teacher over student, employer over employee, police officer over citizen. Often the person with less power believes that the other is acting unfairly. This can lead to feelings of helplessness.

Most have experienced frustration or anger in such instances. Institutions usually provide procedures for reviewing incidents of presumed injustice. The study that follows can be enriched as one reflects on similar cases from personal experience.

A small college offered a course titled "First Aid." The course, scheduled for just six weeks and worth one hour of credit, was one of the options for fulfilling the physical education requirement for graduation. One semester fifty students enrolled in the class, which had a reputation for being an easy, or "cake," course. They joked about how little seemed to be required of them.

The instructor was a first-year assistant football coach who had had some previous teaching experience at a junior college. His outline for the course required students to read a short text-book on first aid. Class time was to be used for general discussion of the assigned chapter topics. But as the weeks went by, the students found that their instructor did not seem to approach the subject material much more seriously than they did. He often took class time to talk about the latest college football game. He seemed to enjoy joking and ribbing the students but did not give them much guidance regarding the course material.

Toward the end of the six weeks, the students were assigned an in-class activity. Each one had to demonstrate his or her ability to wrap a classmate's arm in a sling. The teacher told the students that they would be evaluated on this activity. But some observed that in such a large class he could not check each person's work during a single class period. The only other evaluation for the course was the final exam, a multiple-choice test based on the first-aid text.

Several months later, the students received their semester grades. Many were surprised to discover that they had received a "C" in the course. Students who had otherwise maintained a straight-"A" average throughout college were particularly agitated. After informally comparing the grades they had received, several students wondered whether their grades had been thoughtlessly assigned. They knew they had been evaluated only on the demonstration and the exam.

These students brought the issue to the academic dean, who inquired whether they had spoken to the instructor. Each one had. The dean explained to the students the procedure for challenging the evaluative practices of an instructor. The procedure involved a "hearing" in which a committee of college faculty members would listen to both the students' complaints and the side presented by the teacher. The students pressed for a hearing. The instructor, when asked to give his reasons for assigning grades as he had, replied that he had discarded the exam papers after grading them. He did not have any copies to show the faculty committee.

Upon hearing this, the faculty committee decided that the instructor had insufficient evidence to defend the letter grades. The students were given the option of having their grade changed from "C" to "pass," which would not adversely affect their grade point averages. Many chose this option.

Questions

1. Unmet expectations frequently produce conflict. What might have been the students' unmet expectations for the course? What might have been the instructor's unmet expectations for himself as a teacher and coach?

2. Discuss the advantages and disadvantages of using a committee of college faculty members to hear student complaints. What other options might be available for dealing with student/faculty disagreements?

Treating Others as You wish to Be Treated

Always treat others as you would like them to treat you: that is the Law and the prophets. (Matthew 7:12)

Questions

1. Why is this hard to practice?
2. How can this help in resolving conflicts?
3. How can you think your way into another's thoughts?

19.
A Schoolboy Refuses to Salute the Flag

In recent American history, treatment of the United States flag has prompted much conflict. Many see the flag as a sacred symbol of love and loyalty to the nation. Others regard flag displaying and saluting as idolatrous. Flag issues can be intensely emotional.

The following three incidents portray church people engaged in what today might be considered a form of civil disobedience. In one, a church conference acts as advocate on behalf of an injured member. In another case, dating to World War I, a dissenter appears to have stood alone. In a third case, a group of dissenters are reluctant to accept assistance from a legal-aid agency. These studies raise the question of whether people of conscience should "go it alone" or should accept help from others in confronting authority.

In October of 1930 a Mennonite schoolboy in Newport News, Virginia, touched off community furor when he refused to salute the flag with his classmates. The student, whose family had recently joined a Mennonite church, was supported by his parents. They asked the local school board to exempt him from the flag salute on the basis that it violated his religious principles. The school board agreed and was greeted with vehement protests by individuals and organizations in the community. One society, the Junior Order of United American Mechanics, denounced the action as "dangerous and un-American." They organized a committee to protest the action before the state board of education.

Mennonites interested in the controversy were kept informed through the publication, *Sword and Trumpet*, edited by Mennonite Bishop George R. Brunk. As public protests continued, Brunk acted as a spokesperson and advocate for the Mennonites on the issue throughout the 1930-31 school year. Not everyone in the community felt that the incident portrayed an unpatriotic spirit by the Mennonites. One prominent clergyman, the pastor of the First Presbyterian Church in Newport News, announced his plans to conduct a Sunday evening service on the topic "The Mennonites and Their Faith and History." He invited Bishop Brunk to give the benediction following the message. The pastor gave a statement on the peace-seeking heritage of the Mennonites.

Meanwhile, at least eight organizations in the community protested the school board's action. Some circulated petitions condemning the decision. The school board agreed to meet with representatives of these groups, who submitted petitions that the boy be required to salute the flag.

The chairman of the school board summarized the board's view that the student had acted within his individual rights, and was further protected because neither the U.S. Constitution, the state constitution, nor any state law contained provisions requiring public school students to salute the flag. Another board member, a lawyer, stated that although he belonged to four of the eight organizations protesting the action, he was convinced that the school board had acted properly and in fact had no legal alternative. He added that as far as he could determine, the student had intended no disrespect for the flag or for his country.

Several of the protestors questioned whether the incident was "setting a dangerous precedent." They were convinced that political rather than religious motives had inspired the boy's refusal to conform. Bishop Brunk, who was attending the meeting, explained that the Mennonites had a long heritage of seeking peace and that some considered saluting the flag a militaristic action. He also noted that some Mennonites felt their conscience would not permit them to salute or show deference to an inanimate object other than the cross. No further action was taken by the school board. The controversy continued, however, and Brunk advocated the Mennonites' position in letters to the local newspapers and to the organizations opposing the school board's decision.

Although the student moved from the school district shortly after the incident came to public attention, the Junior Order of United American Mechanics pressed the issue to the state level. The Virginia Mennonite Conference requested that the Mennonites, too, be given a chance to state their position at a hearing before the state board of education. The conference appointed four church leaders, chaired by Brunk, to represent the Mennonite position.

When they arrived in Richmond, the delegation discovered that the Mechanics order, with support from the Ku Klux Klan and the American Legion, had already presented their case. The Mennonites were given the opportunity to speak to the state board, with their opponents in attendance at the hearing. Brunk read a prepared statement highlighting the persecution experienced by the Anabaptists and Mennonites throughout their earlier history. He explained that Mennonite people loved and supported their nation and respected civil authority, but explained that Mennonites as individuals had made varied responses to the call of national duty. He mentioned that during the World War, some Mennonite draftees had served while others had not. Brunk noted later that, though he felt the state board had responded cordially, the meeting grew tense when several lodge members accused him of cowardice and disloyalty.

Brunk and the other Mennonites answered a series of questions. Some involved the denomination's views on Russia and communism. Other questions were hypothetical: "What if all of us in this country believed and acted as you Mennonites do?" Following the meeting, all shook hands. The state board decided to uphold the local school board's decision.

The story of the boy, the flag, and the state school board recalls two earlier cases of refusal to salute the flag. In 1918, the last year of World War I, a man in West Liberty, Ohio, became the first Mennonite prosecuted in a flag-salute case. Ora Troyer had instructed his foster daughter not to participate with her class in the daily flag salute. Several times she was sent home. The local court fined Troyer but he appealed to the Logan County Court of Common Pleas, arguing that he had upheld state laws by sending his foster daughter to school every morning. The judge did not agree, and rebuked Troyer for an act he called "the forerunner of disloyalty and treason."

In 1928, another flag-salute incident took place. Thirty- eight Mennonite schoolchildren in Greenwood, Delaware, were expelled for refusing to salute the flag. Their parents were unsuccessful in convincing local schools to accept the children back, and both the state and local boards argued that the children were violating state flag-salute laws. The American Civil Liberties Union offered to assist the Mennonites by challenging the constitutionality of the laws. But the Mennonites were reluctant to go to court. Instead, they kept their children out of public schools and held private classes in a church basement.

Questions

1. Note that Bishop George R. Brunk acted as a spokesperson and advocate for the Mennonite schoolboy who refused to salute the flag. What is the contribution of the advocate in resolving conflict? Contrast this with the contribution of the impartial mediator.

2. Was the conference's decision to send a delegation to the hearing helpful?

Standing Up For the Accused

The scribes and the Pharisees brought a woman who had been caught in adultery, and placing her in the midst they said to him, "Teacher, this woman has been caught in the act of adultery. Now in the law Moses commanded us to stone such. What do you say about her? This they said to test him, that they might have some charge to bring against him. Jesus bent down and wrote with his finger on the ground. And as they continued to ask him, he stood up and said to them, "Let him who is without sin among you be the first to throw a stone at her." And once more he bent down and wrote with his finger on the ground. But when they heard it, they went away, one by one, beginning with the eldest, and Jesus was left alone with the woman standing before him. Jesus looked up and said to her, "Woman, where are they? Has no one condemned you?" She said, "No one, Lord." And Jesus said, "Neither do I condemn you; go and do not sin again." (John 8:3-7, RSV)

Question

In many conflicts one party has no chance because   he or she lacks power. How did Jesus equalize the power relationships in this situation?

20.
Breaking Down Jim Crow Barriers

The civil rights movement is, among other things, a story of conflict resolution. The movement came in many well-publicized forms: mass nonviolent demonstrations led by Martin Luther King, Jr., and others, court challenges to segregation, and legislative actions. It also came in innumerable local efforts led by courageous, persistent individuals like A. W. Roberson.

Even though it was north of the Mason-Dixon line, Newton, Kansas, was a segregated town until the late 1940s. Blacks were refused meals in all restaurants and drugstores unless they went to the back kitchen door. No black could get a room in a hotel. No Negro child could swim in the public pool. Negroes could not get haircuts in Newton barber shops.

"Negroes," or "colored people," as they were called then, were segregated in the Jim Crow sections of the three movie theaters. Black athletes could play on the high school football team but were barred from the basketball team where black skin would touch white skin. No blacks clerked in stores. Those who were employed worked for the Santa Fe Railroad or as household servants. A few took jobs with the garbage and street departments. At Bethel College black debaters could not be admitted to the national forensic honorary fraternity because the society's national charter forbade "African" members.

Today much of the visible segregation is gone. In part, this is due to court decisions and federal and state civil rights legislation. Changes, however, are also due to persons like A. W. Roberson, a black railway postal clerk who moved to Newton in 1944.

He came from Denison, Texas, and soon after his arrival, near the end of World War II, Mr. Roberson devoted himself to breaking down racial walls. He became president of the small, local branch of the National Association for the Advancement of Colored People (NAACP), which represented the four to five hundred Negroes in Newton. One of his first acts was to apply for NAACP membership in the local Chamber of Commerce in which no black had ever been a member. After a several-month delay, his application for membership was granted. At a Chamber of Commerce dinner he was permitted for the first time to eat in the dining room of the otherwise segregated Ripley Hotel.

Mr. Roberson sought help from the integrated Newton Ministerial Association in opening restaurants and drugstore counters to blacks. He was an active member of a black Baptist church. The chairman of the association expressed his personal goodwill but said that he could not help because many in his congregation came from the South: "I can't get involved. I'll lose my bread and butter." To this Mr. Roberson responded: "But you know it says in the Bible, 'Go ye therefore ... teaching them to observe all things whatsoever I have commanded you: and lo, I am with you alway, even unto the end of the world.' Don't you believe that when you do the right thing, God will take care of you?" The pastor replied, "I guess I have too little faith."

The right of blacks to buy a decent meal in Newton seemed a fundamental right to Mr. Roberson. He and a small mixed group of blacks and sympathetic white friends visited all of Newton's restaurant owners and drugstore counter managers to persuade them to serve blacks. Half of the group started at the south end of Main Street and worked north while the others started at the north end and worked south. In this way every restaurant was visited twice. At the end of the day the two groups compared notes and found that they had been rebuffed at every place. One operator had declared, "Before I'll serve you, I'll close up."

For three years they waited. Mr. Roberson and many others lobbied for a state law to declare such exclusionary practices unlawful. With a new law on the books in the early 1950s they again made their round of Newton restaurants and drugstore counters. No one wanted a lawsuit. Finally, blacks were permitted to sit at the lunch counters in Newton.

One day Mr. Roberson noticed an announcement in the *Newton Kansan* that the Red Cross was sponsoring swimming classes for children at the public swimming pool. He inquired at the pool: "Does this mean all children?" The response was: "I suppose so, but I'd better check." His inquiries led from person to person until he reached the chair of the Red Cross. There he was referred to the city council, which agreed to admit black children if the parents of white children consented. The NAACP had difficulty finding persons who would sign their names, but at the Bethel College Mennonite Church they found twenty-two willing parents. That year Mennonite children in the summer Bible school took swimming lessons alongside black children.

But this was only a partial victory for the blacks, who were still denied use of the large pool. For two years they petitioned that the ban be lifted. Their requests were denied. During the third summer season the NAACP chapter raised a fund for legal fees to sue the city because of this civil rights violation. Mr. Roberson pointed out that blacks were also taxpayers for the public pool. The city proposed a counter offer making provision for the blacks to use the pool on certain days of the week. The NAACP refused this compromise.

Mr. Roberson and his friends then arranged for five black girls, aged ten to fifteen, to go to the pool with bathing suits, towels, and admission money. A group of parents watched discreetly in the background. The girls were refused tickets and told that they would have to go to the city manager for an answer.

The city manager called the city attorney and then called a special council meeting with at least fifteen Negroes in attendance. After the council adjourned to a side room for an executive session, the city attorney advised the council, "We can't stand a suit; we'll lose in court." The mayor came back to publicly affirm, "The council wants to do what is right." The pool was opened to blacks and to Mexicans.

Some had expressed fears that the presence of blacks would lead whites to desert the pool. But on the first day, seventeen blacks and 729 whites came—the largest attendance on record. Since then, the pool has had no incidents between Newton blacks and whites. Mr. Roberson concluded, "There was no black takeover. I don't believe there were ever again so many blacks at the pool on one day." The local newspaper reported nothing about these events.

Mr. Roberson and his wife were also concerned that blacks and Mexicans were confined to a segregated area in the local theater. One evening the couple went to the theater fifteen minutes early, while the bright overhead lights were still on. They went forward and sat in the fifth center row where others could see their blackness. If anyone came to ask them to move, Mr. Roberson planned to say, "Thank you, we are comfortable where we are." Although his wife was a bit uncomfortable, they sat there all evening. No one asked them to move. Mr. Roberson and his wife went to the theater several other times with no adverse action from the management. He then encouraged black friends to go to the theater, to sit forward in the center, and "to be calm, talk nice, keep cool, be quiet, be polite to anyone asking you to move, and don't get angry or use profanity." The blacks agreed in advance that they would have to be carried out if someone made an effort to eject them. There were no incidents. The Jim Crow practices in the Newton theater came to an end.

Mr. Roberson recalls going to a Newton barber shop to have his hair cut. Although the barber was not busy, he refused to give the black man service, stating: "You must have an appointment."

To this Mr. Roberson responded: "You're not refusing to cut my hair, are you?" The barber cut his hair. Mr. Roberson gave the barber a generous tip and commented, "You know, you did a nice job." Years later Mr. Roberson reflected, "People didn't realize that we only wanted to know we could do the things other people could if we wanted to. It's not that we wanted to take over swimming pools, barber shops, and restaurants. We just wanted to be free to do something if we wanted to do it."

Blacks were excluded from the high school basketball team. A black freshman boy, a tall, brilliant basketball player, came with his father to see Mr. Roberson. The student wanted to try out for the high school team. Mr. Roberson went with the father and son to the high school principal, who also served as the basketball coach. The ban was lifted and the boy became a star on the Newton team.

During their first three years in Newton, the Robersons lived with a black plumber. Mr. Roberson recalls their long search for housing. He would call a realtor, who invariably would describe a fine property for sale. When Mr. Roberson went to see the place, the realtor, startled to see a black, would explain unconvincingly, "I'm sorry—since you called, that house is no longer available, but we have a nice little bungalow over on . . . [the black section]." At a tax sale Mr. Roberson bought several lots in a white neighborhood. Soon he was besieged by phone calls from persons wanting to buy the lots to keep a black family out of the neighborhood. But Mr. Roberson found a house northeast of Newton and moved it onto the Newton lot. When it was finally ready for occupancy, a man approached him, saying, "I'll give you twice what you put into it." Mr. Roberson answered, "I'm going to live here and die here." When it came time to move in he took three weeks off from his job to be sure that his family would not be subjected to harassment. Mr. Roberson says that, today, all the people in the neighborhood are his friends: "It shows that people are afraid of the unknown." He adds: "I have always contended that the best way to do away with discrimination is to have people come in contact with each other. They find that they are not too bad."

Mr. Roberson has been asked, "What gives you the courage to live as you have lived, the strength to do what you have done?" He speaks of his family and his church. He also speaks of "the principle of the thing." He goes on to say: "I took that from my daddy. I admired him. He was poor, a laboring man on a railroad maintenance crew. He stood up for what was right. He checked the rails to see whether they were safe. The supervisor once said that they were safe, but Dad stood up and said, 'They're not safe.' I guess I took some of that feeling about right and wrong from my daddy." Mr. Roberson also acknowledges that his federal job with the postal service gave him a base of economic security that protected him from fear of job loss.

Mr. Roberson looks back on his life with satisfaction. "Conditions have changed quite a bit in Newton. I have nice neighbors. However, there is no NAACP chapter now. Things are so much better that people have gotten complacent. Now Newton is more or less integrated with the exception of the churches. It's sad that the church is the last to take a stand. The sports and entertainment worlds were the first to lead out. And yet, I think I could join any church in Newton today."

He speaks of the lessons he has learned: "If you know you're right, don't give up the first time they say 'no.' If you're right, you are likely to get it eventually." Finally, he observes: "I don't believe in violence. Everything can be realized by peaceful means."

Questions

1. Evaluate the various techniques that Roberson and the Newton chapter of the NAACP used in securing equal access: organizing, forming alliances, threatening legal action, protesting nonviolently, responding with politeness. Were some techniques more effective than others? Were some more appropriate than others?

2. Mr. Roberson's experiences involved confrontation and produced nonviolent conflict. Is conflict inevitable when an oppressed group begins to demand better treatment from the dominant group?

Inviting Your Opponent to Join You

He then went off to Tarsus to look for Saul; and when he had found him, he brought him to Antioch. For a whole year the two of them lived in fellowship with the congregation there, and gave instruction to large numbers. It was in Antioch that the disciples first got the name of Christians. (Acts 11:25-26)

Question

How did Barnabas empower the feared Saul to become the trusted colleague Paul?

21.
Befriending Vandals

In nearly every community one sees evidence of vandalism: broken windows, vulgar words painted on public buildings, slashed tires, trash dumped along country roads. The injured party invariably responds with frustration and anger. Rarely does one meet the vandals face-to-face. This case study illustrates a creative response to the destruction of property.

In the southwest sector of Atlanta, Georgia, are twenty-six acres of forest surrounded by residential areas. The forest, known as the Outdoor Activity Center, lies atop historic Bush Mountain. Serving for a year as a Mennonite Central Committee volunteer, I was a naturalist in the Outdoor Activity Center. We conducted nature tours, taught classes, designed exhibits, sold bird feed and sponsored a variety of other nature activities.

Gradually I became acquainted with people from the community surrounding the Outdoor Activity Center. For me, the forest was not just a "work island" in the midst of a residential community but was part of the neighborhood. Children from either side of the center came in after school to talk and joke, refill the bird feeders, and challenge me to bike races down the hill. Winning their friendship was invaluable in reducing maintenance on the buildings and forest.

One month we experienced recurring vandalism in the forest. We discovered young saplings that had been cut down, and later we found a tree fort in a remote section of the forest.

Unable to confront the vandals directly, I typed the following letter, covered it with transparent paper, and tacked it up on the log shelter:

> To the builders of this log shelter:
> I've stopped by a couple of times to talk with you about the construction of this log shelter in the Outdoor Activity Center forest but I could never find you. We are glad that you enjoy using the forest but we are sad that you have cut down trees to make your shelter. This forest is to be enjoyed by everyone and we want to keep it nice and beautiful for all the people of this neighborhood and city. Trees take a long time to grow, and cutting them down makes the forest look ugly. At this point we won't ask you to tear down the log shelter. It can remain and you can use it. We do ask that you pick up any trash or litter you find here and take it to a trash can so that the area remains beautiful. Also, any further cutting in the forest is prohibited and illegal.
> If you have any questions or would like a tour of the exhibit room or forest, or would like to help us at the nature center care for animals or do building projects, stop by and visit. I'd enjoy getting to know you.
> Sincerely,
> Environmental Educator
> P.S. I found an ax and broken shovel by the shelter. Are these yours? If so, you can pick them up from me, either at our offices on Bridges Ave. or at our Richland Road exhibit trailers (where I'll be late afternoons for the rest of the week and also next week).

I didn't expect anything to materialize from this effort. However, a few days later two fourteen-year-old boys, William and Bryant, walked in the door of the center at closing time. They acknowledged that they had built the log tree fort. We spent the next hour looking at the damage that had been done, discussing how it could be corrected, and exploring the forest. I discovered that they were self-taught naturalists who loved the forest and knew every nook and corner. They continued to stop in to observe and visit. William and Bryant became assets to the center.

Questions

1. Evaluate the content and tone of the letter that the naturalist left for the builders of the log shelter. What made it effective?

2. Have persons damaged your property? What are ways in which you can respond to such injury?

Forgiving Others

For if you forgive others the wrongs they have done, your heavenly Father will also forgive you; but if you do not forgive others, then the wrongs you have done will not be forgiven by your Father. (Matthew 6:14-15)

Then Peter came up and asked him, "Lord, how often am I to forgive my brother if he goes on wronging me? As many as seven times?" Jesus replied, "I do not say seven times; I say seventy times seven." (Matthew 18:21-22)

Questions

1. Why is it difficult to forgive?
2. If you forgive, won't they walk over you the next time?

22.
A Mental Health Agency Faces Its Critics

A town is a complex network of relationships. When a new institution enters a community, it can disrupt and realign established patterns.

In this study a county-wide conflict unfolds step by step. It demonstrates that a conflict can involve many groups and institutions, each with particular needs, alliances, and antipathies. Actors in the conflict include an expanding mental health center, its parent office in another city, three county commissioners, a private counseling center, a hospital, the local newspaper, and several citizens' groups. Many communities can report similar experiences.

Beginning in 1965, Valley Psychiatric Center, Inc., of a large Western city, maintained one of several satellite offices fifty miles away in Berryton. The Berryton office sought to serve the mental health needs of Berry County residents, offering counseling and therapy, a wide range of programs related to mental health education, and a substance-abuse program. Because of the limited size of the office staff, the Berryton program focused on prevention and education. Clients who needed prolonged, extensive therapy were referred to Valley Center's main offices in the city.

Berry County is one of the wealthier counties in the state. Berryton, with a population of thirty thousand, is its largest city.

The community boasts a healthy climate for business and industry with well-kept residences, beautiful parks, and an excellent school system. Historically, Berry County has had to maintain a balance of interests between Berryton and smaller communities nearby.

The Valley Center office in Berryton was supported with funds from the Berry County Commission, which acted on the recommendations of a county advisory board on mental health. During the late 1970s a conflict arose over county funding for the institution. A local citizens' group that had organized several years earlier as Advocates of Mental Health Services (AMHS) asked the county commissioners to cut Valley Center's funding on the charge that it was violating a financial disclosure law and thus avoiding fiscal accountability. The group also questioned whether Valley Center's services were meeting the mental health needs of the county. They suggested it was simply "duplicating" already existing programs such as a family counseling center in Berryton. Valley Center, which was completing plans to build a new facility and expand its services in Berryton, argued that AMHS was less concerned with mental health needs than with the political control of county health programs.

In August of 1977 Matthew Davis arrived as the new director of Valley Center's Berryton office. When Davis began his position, the satellite office was located on the second floor of a downtown building. The office staff—convinced that the office lacked accessibility for physically handicapped clients and suffered from inadequate public visibility—explored options for relocating and expanding its facilities. In September of 1977, the county commissioners and interested citizens held a public meeting to discuss the community's mental health needs and Valley Center's opportunities for expansion. Staff members searched for a less expensive location and considered remodeling a house, a vacant hospital, or a hotel, but none of the options emerged as satisfactory.

During this period, Davis and his staff made presentations to clubs and civic organizations, visited schools, and contacted professionals and staff from other Berryton businesses. Davis noticed that while support for the Valley Center program was increasing from many sectors, including other social service agencies, opposition to Valley Center's expansion sharpened. Apparently, some citizens perceived Valley Center as an "outside force" with no legitimate reason to locate in the Berryton community.

In June of 1979 Valley Center began exploring the possibility of opening a halfway house in Berryton. State funding sources encouraged the mental health agency to locate the home in a residential neighborhood. This plan evoked strong resistance from a group of fifty homeowners near the proposed site. They succeeded in having the plan tabled at a zoning board meeting. The incident generated publicity for Valley Center at a time when the mental health agency was coming under sharp attack from AMHS.

Within two weeks of the halfway house incident, Davis was approached by Berryton citizens Warren O'Dell and Stephanie Moore, who questioned him about the agency's plans for expansion. Neither O'Dell nor Moore favored Valley Center presence in the community. Two months earlier, O'Dell had been appointed county commissioner. Moore, the director of a small, private counseling center in the community, tried to persuade the county commissioners to allocate some of the county funds for mental health to her agency. By the time O'Dell and Moore confronted Davis on the expansion issue, Valley Center had decided to purchase property near the hospital and build a new facility.

Davis and other staff members were unprepared, however, for an article which appeared in the July 26 issue of the local paper, the *Berryton News*. It described that day's county commission meeting during which the AMHS had released a twenty-page report questioning Valley Center's fiscal practices and desirability in the community. The article quoted sources critical of Valley Center. A local clinical psychologist, for example, commented on what would happen if Berry County cut off Valley Center's funding:

> As for the local people who are now being counseled by Valley Center, their needs will be met immediately by local resources. This [Berry County] is not Looney Tunes. We will not suddenly have women running naked in the streets or fiends crawling out of hiding places if funds were cut off from Valley Center.

The article also quoted the two county commissioners who had traditionally supported Valley Center. They indicated that they were no longer sure they could support the agency.

In the days following the newspaper article, Valley Center's supporters rallied around the agency. Within the week, at another county commission meeting, twenty-two local residents protested what they considered to be unsubstantiated attacks on Valley Center. They demanded more information on AMHS, which they charged had a secretive and exclusive membership. They asked whether Commissioner O'Dell was directly involved with AMHS.

On August 1, the county commissioners voted two to one to allocate $69,000 for Valley Center's programs in the coming year. O'Dell, the dissenting commissioner, charged that Valley Center had not complied with state financial disclosure laws in the past. He declared his concern for taxpayers and warned that Valley Center deserved close scrutiny. Meanwhile, at the Valley Center main offices fifty miles away, the agency's executive director sent a letter to members of the Berry County mental health advisory board. He expressed dismay at the apparent attempt to discredit and to "trip up" the institution on a technical matter. Valley Center, he emphasized, was making every attempt to comply with the state law on financial disclosure. He affirmed the institution's intentions to remain in Berryton and to expand facilities there to a "more appropriate and permanent location."

During the next month, a series of editorials and letters to the editor on the subject appeared in the *News*. The publisher of the newspaper asserted that Valley Center had not been accountable in the past and should therefore not receive additional funding. Commissioner O'Dell pursued the issue with the state's attorney general, who replied that Valley Center needed to take certain steps to comply with the state law. On the basis of that response, O'Dell moved at the August 27 county commission meeting that Berry County cut all funding to the institution. Neither of the other commissioners seconded the motion. Contrary to indications in the July 22 *News* article, these two commissioners remained supportive of Valley Center.

Matthew Davis and other members of the Valley Center staff were increasingly frustrated at the lack of clarity regarding the agency's future in Berryton. For several years the staff had hoped to expand services and to move into a new building. But it became difficult to work on a day-to-day basis amid uncertainty and recurring attacks on the institution's credibility. The staff saw Valley Center as a pawn in a deep-seated struggle for political power.

A friendly public official explained to Davis that the opposition to the Valley Center facility came from a small group of well-to-do families and firms whose power was declining as local institutions came increasingly under the control of a younger group of professionals and businesspeople. Many Valley Center supporters, meanwhile, urged Davis to push ahead with building plans: "We need Valley Center in our community."

On September 4, Valley Center officials publicly expressed their frustration. Davis and his colleague, Jeanette Swenson, administrator of Valley Center's main office, attended a county commission meeting where Swenson read a prepared statement describing harassment and a "smear campaign" against the institution. Specifically, she named Commissioner O'Dell and AMHS as perpetrators, and she called for citizen response.

Reflecting on this "counter-offensive" move by Valley Center officials, Davis noted later that the Swenson statement had a therapeutic impact on Valley Center staff. The meeting also received some press coverage. Davis and staff members wrote a hundred-page document detailing all relevant aspects of its finances. All three commissioners declared satisfaction with Valley Center's compliance.

In reflecting on the period of controversy, Davis suggested that Valley Center had contributed to its difficulties in Berryton by failing to seek local support from the beginning. Davis felt that the experience with community opposition taught Valley Center a lesson about broadening its bases of support. As a result, Valley Center initiated a series of business and professional luncheons as a public relations effort. During the building process, the agency worked exclusively with local contractors and businesses. Davis felt that such actions of "good faith" helped establish Valley Center as an institution with direct and positive links to the Berryton community.

Even after completion of the new building, critics of Valley Center did not fade away. The following summer, the issue of increased funding emerged again. Opponents argued that Valley Center should not be allowed the large increase recommended by the advisory board while other agencies in the county were facing cuts. Despite vocal opposition and several *News* editorials questioning Valley Center's accountability, the county commissioners voted for the increase in Valley Center's 1981 budget.

Questions

1. Why do you think that Valley Center's expansion provoked such strong opposition from some members of the Berryton community?

2. Do you think the press coverage weakened or strengthened Valley Center's plans for expansion in the community?

3. What conflicts have you witnessed between institutions in the local community, such as competition between two hospitals, conflict between city and county governments, or the consolidation of schools?

Challenging the Oppressor

You have learned that they were told, "Eye for eye, tooth for tooth." But what I tell you is this: Do not set yourself against the man who wrongs you. If someone slaps you on the right cheek, turn and offer him your left. If a man wants to sue you for your shirt, let him have your coat as well. If a man in authority makes you go one mile, go with him two. Give when you are asked to give; and do not turn your back on a man who wants to borrow. (Matthew 5:38-42)

Questions

1. Who should make the first move?

2. Does this passage square with the comment "My door is always open whenever they want to make peace"?

3. Is Jesus urging us to seize the initiative?

23.
A Community Opposes a Uranium Refinery

Every community must grapple with controversial issues that pit economic factors against consideration of quality of life. Such issues might revolve around the following: establishing a military base, providing a place to deposit hazardous waste, setting up tax inducements to attract an industry, granting permission to the developers of a gambling enterprise, or protecting land for environmental purposes. Communities need to weigh carefully the short- and long-term effects of major programs. Individuals who raise questions are often unable to resist powerful, well-funded forces. This case study highlights church groups and other community members who succeeded in building a coalition of concern.

In the spring of 1976 a group of officials from the Saskatchewan Economic Development Corporation arrived in Warman, Saskatchewan. They wanted to purchase land east of town for what they called a "satellite city" or "industrial complex." Citizens of Warman, a community with a population of more than one thousand people, located in the midst of a concentration of Mennonites, soon learned that Eldorado Nuclear Limited, a federal crown (government) corporation, wanted to build a $100 million uranium refinery in the area.

Uranium, mined and processed in northern Saskatchewan,

was to be refined at the Warman plant into uranium hexafluoride. This form of the chemical would be exported to Europe and developing nations as fuel for nuclear power plants, or to the United States for further enrichment and use in U.S. power plants. Since Canada's nuclear reactors could not use the uranium hexafluoride, all of the refinery's production was destined for export.

Eldorado proposed building its third refinery in Saskatchewan in order to have processing facilities close to its northern Saskatchewan mining operations. Eldorado's existing refinery and one refinery under construction were both located in Ontario. But since the uranium resource was indigenous to Saskatchewan, local government and business groups hoped that the wealth from processing it could remain in their own province.

Many Saskatchewan residents believed that the Warman refinery would bring a boom to the Warman and Saskatoon economies. Proponents of the refinery pointed out that the $100 million project would provide 390 construction jobs and would create two hundred permanent jobs. In addition, from thirty to forty million dollars would be spent locally during construction. Most members of the business community considered construction of the refinery essential to the economic growth of Saskatchewan. The Atomic Energy Control Board, the Saskatchewan Economic Development Corporation, the North West Economic Development Council, and the town councils of surrounding towns and rural municipalities joined in support of the refinery.

Opposition to the proposed refinery was also broadly based. Environmental groups such as the Saskatoon Environmental Society and the Saskatoon Citizens for a Non-Nuclear Society joined with the National Farmers Union, a number of church groups, some local business managers and elected officials, and 250 local farm families in opposing the proposal. The most vocal opposition group was the Warman and District Concerned Citizens Group (WDCCG), a loosely organized "grass-roots" organization with over eight hundred members. Ninety percent of these individuals lived near the proposed site. The original objective of the WDCCG, which had formed in 1977 in response to Eldorado's announced interest in the Warman area, was to educate the community about the refinery. Soon the organization's focus shifted to opposing the refinery.

In March of 1979 the membership of the WDCCG increased a dramatic 300 percent, rising to five hundred members. The organization had established credibility within the community. Hoping to avoid identification as a placard-waving anti-nuclear organization, the WDCCG avoided bumper stickers, mass demonstrations, and petitions. The WDCCG focused on initiating dialogue with farmers, Warman residents, and local public officials. As one WDCCG member stated, "Everyone was considered a potential ally to be reached by gentle and effective persuasion."

The WDCCG tried to be sensitive to the varied social and political views of its members. It was careful not to identify itself with a particular party or certain candidates. The association embraced persons with diverse perspectives on agricultural land use, stewardship of resources, weapons proliferation, radioactive waste, pollution, and economic factors.

The proposal to establish the Warman refinery required a long, complex process. Eldorado submitted an Environmental Impact Statement to the Federal Environmental Review Office. This agency then appointed an Environmental Assessment Panel responsible for receiving briefs, holding public hearings, and making recommendations on the proposal to the federal Minister of the Environment. The final decision would be made by the federal cabinet.

Public hearings were held for twelve days in January of 1980. Although the hearings were scheduled for only nine days, an extra three were added to accommodate the large public response. During the hearings more than three thousand pages of transcripts were produced and 226 citizens voiced opposition to the refinery. Thirty-four persons spoke in favor of it.

The Environmental Assessment Panel released its recommendations in mid-August of 1980. The panel did not endorse the proposed Warman site for the refinery because of the potential social impact on the local community, "a distinctive community (which) exists in the vicinity of the impact area ... uniquely associated with the Mennonite ethnic and religious community."

The panel outlined several alternatives that would satisfy regulations prior to a decision on the refinery site: 1) Eldorado must provide further information on the social impact of the proposal, including the extent to which the presence of a uranium refinery might erode the community's religious beliefs, the extent to which the concept of stewardship occurred locally, and the effects of refinery encroachment on agricultural activities. This new information would be subject to further public review. 2) Eldorado must select an alternative site in Saskatchewan, evaluating the social and environmental impact of a refinery on the area. This information would also be subject to public review.

In response to the panel's findings, Eldorado chose not to renew its land options at the Warman site. The corporation felt that it could not gain approval for the site within the designated one-year period because of the social-impact studies required.

A number of other Saskatchewan communities began to express interest in having Eldorado locate in their area. One was the community of Langham, located approximately fifteen miles west of Warman. Like Warman, Langham had congregations of General Conference Mennonites and Evangelical Mennonite Brethren.

Although the refinery's opponents were pleased that the refinery was not given the "go-ahead," many people felt that the panel's report did not accurately reflect the hearings. They charged that the panel focused on Mennonites and used Eldorado's failure to study the social impact on the Mennonite culture as a scapegoat, while ignoring the environmental impact and the fact that numerous other church, union, and public-interest groups had also opposed the refinery.

While the merits of the refinery were being debated, Mennonite responses were mixed. Most Mennonite churches did not take a stand on the controversial proposal. A large number of Mennonites felt that the issue had no place within the church. Warman's mayor, a Mennonite Brethren, stated that the issue had not come up in his church: "It causes division if you bring issues like that into the church." As mayor, however, he presented a pro-refinery brief at the hearings on behalf of the Warman town council, emphasizing the economic benefits the refinery would bring.

Two local Mennonite churches, Osler Mennonite Church and Bergthaler Mennonite Church, addressed the issue. The Osler congregation's 1977 resolution calling for a moratorium on nuclear development was reaffirmed overwhelmingly in 1979, before the hearings began. The pastor of this church also served as the chair for the WDCCG. Bergthaler Mennonite Church, with Rev. John D. Reddekop as its spokesperson, stated:

> Mennonites believe that the way people can find fellowship is in caring for each other physically and spiritually. It's against our conscience to consent to atomic weapons that could later be used to destroy the human race.

Some residents of Warman felt that the controversy had had a negative impact on the community: "People were divided in their views, certain church tensions occurred, and generally an unhealthy atmosphere prevailed." Even so, there were many positive effects on the community during the four-year struggle against the refinery. A dairy farmer, looking back over the years of controversy, stated:

> Our community, like a community faced with a disaster such as a flood, has experienced some damage, but we have joined together and have come through. The feelings of the community are stronger, and we are better prepared to express what shape we would like our community to take.

Questions
1. What made WDCCG an effective advocacy group?
2. Note that "most Mennonite churches did not take a stand on the controversial proposal." Why didn't they?
3. Identify other conflicts in which proponents of economic development clash with advocates of environmental protection or social values. What role, if any, should the church take in such community conflicts?

The "Quick Fix" or the Renunciation of Violence

As the time approached when he was to be taken up to heaven, he set his face resolutely towards Jerusalem, and sent messengers ahead. They set out and went into a Samaritan village to make arrangements for him; but the villagers would not have him because he was making for Jerusalem. When the disciples James and John saw this they said, "Lord, may we call down fire from heaven to burn them up?" But he turned and rebuked them, and they went on to another village. (Luke 9:51-56)

Question
Is this "quick fix" to an annoying problem similar to social and political proposals today?

Striking in Self-Defense

At that moment one of those with Jesus reached for his sword and drew it, and he struck at the High Priest's servant and cut off his ear. But Jesus said to him, "Put up your sword. All who take the sword die by the sword." (Matthew 26:51-52)

Question
What satisfactions and harm may come from an impulsive, violent retaliation?

24.
Jim's Struggle to Save the Farm

Early in this century most Americans lived on farms and in small towns. Farmers raised a variety of crops and livestock, but since then, farming has become highly specialized. Agri-businesses are rapidly displacing small farmers. The family farm is an endangered species.

In the late 1970s and throughout the 1980s, many farmers were faced with bankruptcy. This case study is rooted in the frustration of independent farmers caught in a rapidly changing economy.

During the spring of 1972, when Jim Bauer was a senior in college, his father died unexpectedly of a heart attack at the age of forty-six. Jim, who already had signed a contract to teach and coach in a western Kansas high school following graduation, was asked by his mother to take over the family farm of 320 acres. Although Jim had always enjoyed farming, he had considered it a remote career possibility because it would be another fifteen years before his father would be ready to retire. Jim knew he would not have the capital to start farming on his own.

Jim's two older twin sisters were married and lived out of state. They encouraged Jim to take charge. Jim's father had owned 320 acres of central Kansas land debt-free and had ample buildings and equipment. He had also rented four hundred acres and fed about one hundred head of cattle. A week after commencement Jim married Jean, his college sweetheart. He secured release from his teaching contract. After a weekend honeymoon, Jim and Jean moved onto the home place and prepared for the harvest. Meanwhile, Jim's mother had purchased and moved into a house in a nearby town.

Jim came to the family farm at a time of rising grain and cattle prices. A year after his father's death, Jim had the opportunity to buy 320 acres of adjoining land. He and his mother took out a first mortgage on the family's 320 acres and this additional land. Jim, aware of the world food crisis, sought to expand his production. He obtained a loan to install irrigation systems on 320 acres, and a year later he borrowed again to build a barn for hog production. Although the interest rates were high, everything looked encouraging as wheat and hog prices rose. Jim and his mother, who cosigned the mortgage papers for this expansion, hoped to pay off the debts in ten to fifteen years.

But then wheat prices plunged to half of the earlier levels, the hog market collapsed, and diesel fuel and fertilizer costs increased sharply. Jim was barely meeting expenses and payments on the loans. Although his family was supportive, his promising life on the farm was beginning to cave in. Jim felt that he was the victim of forces beyond his control. As his financial crisis deepened, he began to take note of the American Agricultural Movement meetings in his county.

The American Agriculture Movement (AAM) was born in September 1977 in a Springfield, Colorado, cafe near the Kansas border. A group of farmers, angered by the low prices they received for farm commodities, agreed to strike if nothing was done about the situation. The farmers sought federal action to guarantee 100 percent parity on certain farm commodities. Parity calls for equivalent purchasing power today for selected farm commodities in comparison to the base years of 1910-14.

The farmers warned that they would not plant or market crops in 1978 unless parity prices were assured. The idea spread like a prairie grass fire. A few days later, strike apostles began carrying their message to nearby towns in Colorado and Kansas. They called the movement a "Farm Strike":

> We, the American farmers, are demanding 100 percent of parity for all agricultural products.... This proposal is being presented to all existing agricultural organizations in the United States. If these organizations do not endorse and support this proposal, we will cancel all memberships.... This ultimatum is also being presented to the Congress of the United States with our deadline Dec. 14, 1977, for action. If this proposal is not enacted into law by our deadline, we will strike. We will not plant our crops in 1978.

Handbills rolled off the presses and mimeographs. Bumper stickers appeared: "If You Don't Like Wheat Farmers, Don't Talk with Your Mouth Full," "We Support the Family Farm," "We Support Agricultural Strike." Rhetoric poured out: "Our proposals are reasonable. Our goals are obtainable. Our ultimatum is justified. We ask your support. Strike for your homes, farms, ranches, and businesses. Strike with the same dedication you have long employed to make this the greatest food-producing nation the world has ever known." Again and again the strikers declared: "We will not advocate violent action. We will not condone violence but ... *we will strike.*" The language was strong: "demand," "deadline," "strike."

Out of curiosity, Jim attended several local meetings. He found that the group's enthusiasm lifted his spirits, and several friends urged him to provide leadership. The farm strike movement, in its first weeks of rapid growth in October, November, and December of 1977, exuded a confidence that intense effort would lead to victory. Such contagious excitement had qualities of a religious revival. The movement took pride in its anti-establishment image. There were claims of "no memberships, no dues, no secretaries, no presidents." Strike centers sprang up in mobile homes, in empty storefronts, and in spare spaces of implement firms. In Kansas, strikers established 110 centers. Some strikers spent hundreds of dollars to carry the message to neighboring towns and even all the way to Washington, D.C.

Jim learned that although there were many common denominators, each strike headquarters seemed to have its own style. Symbols included the tractor, the visor cap, bumper stickers, jackets with farm strike patches, and caucusing in roadside cafes. Some in the movement expressed hostility toward existing organizations such as the American Farm Bureau. Hostility also focused on the Secretary of Agriculture, the President, and the "they" of large multinational corporations.

Jim liked the way in which the farm strike movement emphasized the image of the family farm. On one two-hour fundraising Farm Strike Telethon, strike organizers used old-fashioned symbols such as windmills, lanterns, oil lamps, and rail fences as background props. The movement was also quick to employ new tactics and technology. Jim was uncomfortable with some of the methods of the movement. The demonstrations of the 1960s may have provided ideas for dramatizing concerns. Long caravans drove into county-seat towns, and tractors circled statehouses. Demonstrators rode buses to Washington for sit-ins in federal buildings, to picket and to distribute handbills. Some farm lobbyists organized boycotts of retail chains and publicized food gifts to striking coal miners. In the spring of 1978 a call came for all farmers to join in a "plowdown," that is, plowing up newly seeded fields. This strike tactic, which captured public attention in the early months of the American Agriculture Movement, alienated many. Later the method was deliberately de-emphasized in AAM literature.

Originally, the American Agricultural Movement demanded a federal guarantee of 100 percent parity on certain commodities. Later, striking farmers accepted a modified position when, in March of 1978, the United States Senate passed the "flexible parity" emergency farm bill introduced by Kansas Senator Robert Dole. The bill was defeated in the House of Representatives three weeks later by a 119-vote margin. Striking farmers, who descended on Washington by the thousands to lobby for the Dole farm bill, were disappointed, frustrated, and angry.

Jim was invited to join a group of AAM farmers going to Washington to voice their grievances and their support for the bill. He was tempted to go with them, but feelings of independence prevailed and he backed away. He had problems on the farm that needed attention.

Several weeks after the House vote on the Dole bill, Jim and Jean spent an evening in discussion with two couples who had gone to Washington. One person commented: "Let's face it. Except for the farm state senators and congressmen, we have few advocates." Another added: "Farmers are divided; we don't speak with one voice. It's small grain farmers versus cattlemen, renters versus owners, part-timers versus full-timers, young farmers with debts versus older farmers who have no big debts, dairymen versus cotton farmers versus orchard growers." One observed: "I once loved to have land prices go up. Every year I felt richer and richer and could borrow more and more. Now I'm not so sure it was good to have all those city people buying up land and driving up the prices." Another lamented, "If we could only go back to farming as it was in the days of my grandfather. Today only the big corporations can compete in the fast lane of high technology and heavy dependence on oil."

Most of the conversation that evening was melancholy in tone. The three couples avoided talking explicitly about their own problems. Everyone in the room knew, however, that everyone was in trouble. Toward the end of the evening Jim commented: "Every successful movement has to build a coalition with other groups. If farmers want to succeed politically and economically they are going to have to put together a coalition with other interest groups. Two percent of the population can't go it alone."

Meanwhile, Jim and Jean were preoccupied day and night with the problems of saving the farm. They tried to pull their resources together in order to meet the quarterly payments on the loans at the bank. Jim cut back his hog operations and sold a tractor and other equipment at far less than he had paid for it. His mother found a job in a school cafeteria because he couldn't meet his rental payments to her. The banker who had been so friendly and encouraging seemed grim and less understanding, and intimated the possibility of foreclosure if payments were not made on time. Both Jim and Jean renewed their teaching licenses and found jobs teaching in high school. This new income was barely enough to meet the quarterly payments on loans.

Jim dreaded going to see the banker, but finally asked whether the loan payment schedule could be adjusted to ease the burden. The banker explained: "I know it's tough, and I sympathize, but the bank is in a tight bind with the auditors who look carefully at our heavy load of farm loans. We might make adjustments for you, but we would also have to do it for others. Then the bank could be in deep trouble."

Jim felt bad because he thought he had failed his mother, who had risked her financial future by cosigning for the loans on land, equipment and buildings. He feared he had disappointed his sisters, whom he knew had hopes of an eventual family inheritance from the farm. Both Jim and Jean were working long hours trying to farm and hold down teaching positions. They had postponed having a family. Jim began to find it difficult to talk with Jean about their financial problems. They seemed blocked in every effort to keep afloat financially.

Finally a month came when they could not make the full quarterly payment on the loans. Jim considered filing for bankruptcy, but was ashamed to propose the possibility. He wondered to whom he could go to talk about the family's problems. Their pastor? A lawyer? Old college friends?

Questions

1. Note Jim's judgment that the American Agricultural Movement lacked cohesiveness and a sense of hope. What factors contributed to these problems?

2. If Jim and Jean lived in your community and were active members of your congregation, to whom could they turn for help?

3. In the current farm crisis, mediation between farmers and creditors is gaining wider acceptance. How might trained mediators help farmers in financial trouble?

Love Your Enemies

You have learned that they were told, "Love your neighbour, hate your enemy." But what I tell you is this: Love your enemies and pray for your persecutors; only so can you be children of your heavenly Father, who makes his sun rise on good and bad alike, and sends the rain on the honest and the dishonest. If you love only those who love you, what reward can you expect? Surely the tax-gatherers do as much as that. (Matthew 5:43-46)

Questions

1. Do you have an enemy?

2. In what ways can you love a personal enemy or a national enemy?

3. How can praying for persecutors help in resolving conflict? For what should one pray?

25.
The School Board Fires a Teacher

The firing of teachers, coaches, and principals is often among the least noble chapters in a community's history. Generally, conflicts over firing are related less to black-and-white issues than to shades of gray. This case study invites one to consider balancing firmness and fairness. It also invites one to reflect on how concerned citizens should intervene if public officials appear to be in error.

Controversy erupted one spring in a small community in the Pacific northwest when Hugh Gardner, a fifteen-year veteran of the town's high school teaching faculty, learned that his contract would not be renewed for the following school year. Gardner was an exuberant history and journalism instructor who set high academic standards for his students. A towering figure (six feet, six inches tall), rigorous in student discipline and highly creative, Gardner had won both admirers and detractors during his teaching career. His most celebrated teaching technique was to play the role of a historical character such as Henry VIII, Abraham Lincoln, or General George Patton, complete with costume and props.

A man with flamboyant style who spoke his convictions, Gardner was not new to controversy. But his previous experiences did not prepare him for the morning when a colleague took him aside and said, "Hugh, I get the feeling that you don't know what's going on." The teacher friend then told him that a petition with from thirty to forty signatures, asking for Gardner's dismissal, had been circulated throughout the community.

The parents of two of Gardner's students had drafted the petition. The parents, respected members of the community, objected to the teacher's "intimidating style and browbeating ways." When Gardner learned the identity of those who were circulating the petition, he observed, "It must have started when their kids received C's in semester finals. The parents expected them to receive A's." What distressed Gardner most was that the parents were members of his congregation and had not spoken to him about their call for his release.

Later in the week Gardner received confirmation of the news when the superintendent of schools delivered a letter authorized by the school board. The letter stated that Gardner would not be rehired and charged that he had "repeatedly displayed insubordination . . . [and] failed to cooperate with other teachers and the school administration in such matters as the establishment of [a new history curriculum]. . . ." The school board charged further that Gardner had displayed "unprofessional conduct" through inappropriate language, unjustifiable grading practices, and public humiliation of students.

Both the principal and the superintendent had complained previously about Gardner's independent style. The principal quoted to the board the words of one teacher, "I don't see why we have to submit lesson plans when Gardner submits them only when he feels like it." Gardner admitted that sometimes he was irritated at the principal because the latter rarely talked to him personally but instead "sent testy little memos." Gardner added, "If only he had sat down with me and explained his reasons, I would have played ball, reluctantly perhaps, but played ball."

Gardner, unhappy with the school board's action, asked for a hearing, to which he was entitled under state education guidelines. The hearing committee consisted of three persons, one chosen by Gardner; a second chosen by the school board; a third, the chair, designated by the first two members. Gardner took a two-week leave of absence from the classroom and discussed with friends and church members how best to handle the situation. Gardner, at the age of forty, felt that his options for finding alternative employment were limited. He maintained that he had conducted himself in a professional manner but that his methods did differ at times from those approved by the school administration. Gardner attributed this to his commitment to improving the educational system.

To his friends and family he confided his distress at the rumors floating about town. One was that he had forced some students to attend an X-rated movie with him. Another was that teachers who testified for or against him at the forthcoming hearing might expect repercussions. Said Gardner: "The rumors hurt most. How does one defend oneself?"

Prior to the hearing, Gardner's pastor attempted to negotiate between the school administration and the teacher. The pastor proposed that Gardner be given a contract for the following year on the condition that he meet weekly with a group from his church to examine the criticisms regarding his teaching. The pastor explained that through group discernment, both the community and church might turn a potentially destructive confrontation into an experience of growth. He found Gardner ready to discuss the proposition, but school administrators refused to consider it. The disappointed pastor concluded that "the community has told the church to stay out of it."

A second attempt at negotiation followed. A local businessman who had served previously on the school board proposed to board members that they rescind their earlier decision, offer Gardner a contract, clear his file, and state publicly that the matter had been resolved. For his part, Gardner must agree verbally that he would not accept the contract offered for the following school year. But neither the board nor the teacher accepted this alternative plan.

One of the school board members admitted off the record to a local newspaper reporter that the board decision had been divisive. This board member, who had voted for Gardner's release, now had second thoughts about the action:

> Maybe we relied too heavily on the judgment of the principal and superintendent, who may not have handled the whole thing too well. Gardner is a bit of a pain in the neck but he is a good pain in the neck. And yet, unless there is clear reason not to, a board has to back up its administrators on close decisions.

That spring, as the date of the hearing approached, the Gardner controversy remained a prime topic of discussion among townspeople. The local newspaper reported on developments related to the case and printed a flood of letters submitted by Gardner's former students who supported the teacher. While much of the local controversy centered on personality factors and Gardner's teaching record, school board members increasingly found themselves on the defensive for their decision to "do what is best for the students." As the hearing neared, one person close to the case warned that "the community will be torn apart when this thing goes public. Neighbors will be called on to testify on opposite sides of the issue. All kinds of people will be hurt in the end."

Questions

1. List and discuss problems that might produce conflict between a teacher and a school administration.

2. Note that Gardner's pastor attempted to negotiate between the school administrators and Gardner. Why do you think the school administrators refused to discuss the pastor's offer?

3. Design a mediation plan that the school and Gardner might both accept. Who might serve as mediator?

Meddling in Another's Quarrel

Like a man who seizes a passing cur by the ears
is he who meddles in another's quarrel.
A man who deceives another
and then says, "It was only a joke,"
is like a madman shooting at random
his deadly darts and arrows.
For lack of fuel a fire dies down
and for want of a tale-bearer a quarrel subsides.
Like bellows for the coal and fuel for the fire
is a quarrelsome man for kindling strife.
A gossip's whispers are savoury morsels
gulped down into the inner man.
Glib speech that covers a spiteful heart
is like glaze spread on earthenware.
With his lips an enemy may speak you fair
but inwardly he harbors deceit;
when his words are gracious, do not trust him,
for seven abominations fill his heart;
he may cloak his enmity in dissimulation,
but his wickedness is shown up before the assembly.
(Proverbs 26:17-26)

Question

What tips does the writer of Proverbs offer on the art of managing conflicts?

GLOSSARY

CONFLICT RESOLUTION PROCESSES

Negotiation
: Process of conferring with another party to come to terms over a conflict of interest. Two or more conflicting parties join in a temporary bargaining relationship to exchange information about their interests, to exchange resources, or to agree on new relationships.

Mediation
: An informal, voluntary process often used when there is an ongoing relationship among family members, neighborhood, or community. A mediator is a neutral party who assists the disputants in communicating issues of the dispute and who aids them in reaching a mutually acceptable agreement.

Conciliation
: Process of preparing parties psychologically to discuss the issues causing conflict. The process is designed to improve communications and to encourage trust.

Arbitration
: Process of determining a solution to a controversy by a third party chosen or accepted by the contending parties.

Bargaining
: Process of making substantive, procedural, or psychological trade-offs to settle a conflict.

Adjudication
: A formal process in an adversarial setting in which a decision is rendered by a judge based on consideration of evidence and application of law to facts.

FORMS OF CONFLICT

Conflict
: A natural part of human experience in which two or more parties believe they have incompatible objectives

(for example, power or limited resources) leading them to try to hurt, subdue, or neutralize the other party.

Argument
: A discussion where two or more parties seek to convince or persuade each other.

Debate
: A discussion between opponents who seek to convince the other to see things as he or she does.

Dispute
: A debate which moves into a more formal setting calling for mediation, conciliation, or arbitration.

Game
: A situation where one seeks to outwit one's opponent, maximizing wins and minimizing losses. In both debates and games the opponent is essential; therefore, in a sense, opponents cooperate.

Fight
: A conflict where the opponent is eliminated, humiliated, subjugated, or driven away. Therefore, one views the opponent irrationally and with fear.

Quarrel
: A general term covering varieties of conflict between or among antagonists, implying a verbal clash followed by strained or severed relationships. Similar terms are wrangle, suggesting noisy, persistent dispute; altercation, suggesting childish dispute; spat, suggesting a lively but brief dispute over a trifle; and tiff, suggesting a brief, inconsequential dispute over a trifle.

INTERVENTION ROLES

Activist
: A leader who identifies with one of the conflicting parties and speaks and acts as a partisan of that party.

Advocate
: An individual who identifies with one party but draws on a broader perspective than the partisan position.

Mediator
: A third party, acceptable to the conflicting parties, who seeks to achieve a win/win resolution of a conflict by facilitating communication, aiding negotiation, identifying additional options, and formulating mutually satisfactory settlements.

Researcher
: An independent fact-finding person who provides information useful to the process of resolving a conflict.

Enforcer
: An independent power, often representing the government, who requires specified behavior of the conflicting parties.

Ombudsperson A third party who investigates citizens/government, client/service provider, or employee/employer complaints in order to resolve a dispute. Sometimes this third party proposes responsive changes in the system.

OTHER TERMS

Active
Listening
Listening intensely for both the content and the emotional quality of a message and then reflecting it back to the speaker to verify accuracy.

Avoidance
A negotiator follows a strategy of non-response or non-engagement in a conflict as a means of preventing an undesirable or untimely settlement.

Brain-
storming
An idea-sharing session where participants, agreeing to postpone all criticism and evaluation of ideas, freely generate ideas and options without pausing to evaluate whether they are realistic or unrealistic, good or bad.

Caucus
A private meeting of members of one party in a conflict to decide strategies for the joint sessions.

Common
Interests
Relational, procedural, or psychological needs that are held jointly by conflicting parties.

Compromise
A midway solution which both sides in a conflict can accept.

Contract
A formal agreement resulting from negotiations that specifies commitments and exchanges.

Face-saving
The need of a person to maintain one's position or image in a negotiation or agreement while at the same time reconciling that with previously stated principles or past deeds.

Facilitate
A third party helps the conflicting parties to communicate, exchange information, or negotiate.

Impasse
A deadlock or stalemate of negotiations in which the parties in conflict are unable to move toward settlement.

Interests
One party's needs, desires, concerns, fears, and hopes. Interests are not to be confused with position, in which one decides to take a stand. Interests may or may not be best represented in a particular position taken.

Position	A person's stated solution to the problem.
Positional Bargaining	A negotiation process in which a series of positions—ranging from a first proposal with a large demand to other proposals with lesser demands—are presented to the opponent.
Power	The ability to assert influence over another person or persons.
Storytelling	Each party in a conflict has opportunity to present in an uninterrupted way from their perspective the whole situation from beginning to end.
Timing	Awareness of and use of the right moments to begin negotiations and make offers.

ROLE PLAYING

A role play is an improvised drama in which the players take on roles in a given situation as preparation for encountering a similar situation or evaluating a past one.

PURPOSE: To try out and analyze situations, theories, and tactics. To understand people and their roles. To develop insights into the thoughts and feelings of "opponents." To anticipate new situations. To reveal fears, anxieties, and other feelings persons have about an action.

DESCRIPTION:

1. *Select a situation:* Most of the case studies in this volume can be used for role playing. Other situations—particularly simple ones in which problems have possible solutions—can be designed for dramatization by the group. Remember that a role play is not a psychodrama, a form of therapy in which a person acts out with others situations related to his or her own problems, maintaining his or her own identity. In a role play, one acts out roles in a conflict situation, assuming an identity other than one's own.

2. *Explain the situation:* All participants should first read the case study. The leader summarizes briefly the conflict situation.

3. *Cast roles:* The leader asks for volunteers or urges persons to assume roles that they do not identify with strongly. It is helpful if participants take fictitious names.

4. *Prepare role players:* Allow a few minutes for persons to get into their roles, decide on their general perspective, and plan their strategy. Ask participants to think of other aspects of their roles (job, family, motivations) to make the roles real. Persons are encouraged to avoid stereotypes in planning the roles.

5. *Prepare observers:* Observers are used when groups are too large for all to participate directly. Suggest that observers watch for language, gestures, revealing comments, and changes in the flow of the conflict.

6. *Set the scene:* The leader establishes the scene, the physical layout, and other relevant details.

7. *The role play itself:* The leader may ask for a minute of silence so participants can get into their roles. The observers are encouraged to listen and observe carefully.

8. *Cut:* The leader stops the role play when enough issues have been uncovered, the action comes to a logical end, or participants want to stop. The leader should intervene if someone becomes unduly distressed or if the role play dissolves into laughter. If participants don't seem 'into' their roles, the leader should cut and redefine the situation. If a person over-identifies with a role (indicated by evidence of great tension), the role play should be cut and the person helped to step out of the role.

9. *Short break:* Participants take a break of a minute or less and move out of the location used in the role play. If the experience was tense, the leader can help release tension by suggesting a quick game, stretch, song, or refreshments.

10. *Evaluation:* Participants and observers have the opportunity to assimilate what took place. If the leader is accepting of ideas, is able to say, "I don't know," but is ready to contribute, the learning process will be stimulating. Leaders should invite examination of (a) feelings and tensions, (b) tactics and goals, and (c) theory and application. Begin by asking the role players how they felt in their roles. Ask observers for their impressions. Refer to characters by the names used in the role play so that individuals do not begin to express hostility or take criticism personally.

Discourage negative evaluation of participants as to what they should have done. Mistakes made during role plays are excellent sources for learning. Comments that encourage role players include: "Another option that you might try is ... ." "Perhaps this would work if ... ." "Judging from the response you received, another tactic that might be used is. . . . ."

The evaluation should not go on too long.

11. *Summation:* The leader facilitates a sense of accomplishment within the group. Participants may be asked to list new insights and new

solutions that have occurred to them in the role play.

(Adapted and abridged from the *Resource Manual for a Living Revolution*, published by New Society Publishers, 4722 Baltimore Ave., Philadelphia, PA 19143.) Used by permission.

GUIDELINES AND MODELS FOR UNDERSTANDING CONFLICT

Many excellent handbooks are available on the art of conflict resolution. (Consult the section "For Further Study.") Each book offers unique perspectives on the peacemaking task. Following are models—windows of understanding—that suggest different ways of analyzing and responding to group conflicts.

1. MOVING FROM LOSE-LOSE TO WIN-WIN

David Augsburger, in *Caring Enough to Confront,* offers this self-explanatory diagram on the varied win-lose alternatives in conflicts.

SEE DIAGRAM ON OPPOSITE PAGE ━━━▶

2. THE STAGES OF PEACEMAKING

Many conflicts are caused by imbalanced relationships of power. One person is strong and the other is weak, one controls information and the other is uninformed, one is an insider and the other is an outsider, one is well-to-do and the other is poor. The peacemaker seeks to understand both the role of power and the individuals' awareness of these relationships.

Each of the different stages of a conflict requires a distinct peacemaking approach. To help balance the relationships between conflicting

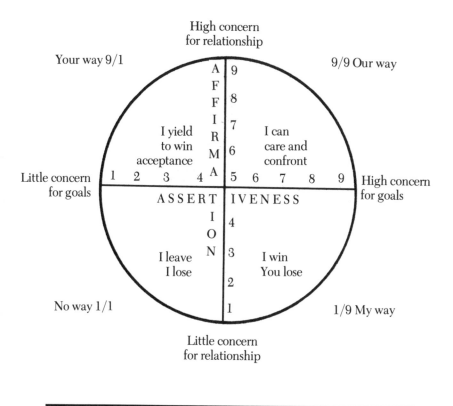

parties, the peacemaker may need to encourage open expression of conflict. Sometimes advocacy of one party must precede mediation. John Paul Lederach has adapted a diagram from Adam Curle's *Making Peace* to show the stages of conflict and various peacemaking responses. This model suggests how peacemaking is more than technique; it must be rooted in concern for justice.

UNPEACEFUL RELATIONS   PEACEFUL
                                             RELATIONS

	Lower Awareness of Conflict	Higher Awareness of Conflict	
Balanced Relations (equal power)		3. Techniques of conciliation and bargaining, applied to end the open conflict and for agreement on a settlement	4. Restructuring of the formerly unpeaceful relations
Unbalanced Relations (unequal power)	1. Various forms of education to increase awareness to the point of confrontation	2. Various techniques of confrontation aimed at reducing the imbalance and enabling the underdogs to negotiate on a basis of greater equality	

3. CONFLICT INTENSITY AND DEPTH OF COMMUNICATION

In the midst of disagreement we find our emotions rising as the intensity increases. This paralyzes our ability to listen and to speak. John Paul Lederach, adapting a diagram from Richard E. Walton's *Interpersonal Peacemaking*, charts the relationship between conflict intensity and depth of communication. He observes that the most dynamic groups are those that have the maximum conflict they can handle constructively. These groups hover around point B. The least dynamic are those that move quickly from point A to C.

Point A represents low intensity in a relationship, little interaction and expression of differences, and a superficial level of communication and understanding.

Point B represents the ideal, the maximum level of conflict intensity and emotional involvement that can be handled productively. However, there is a limit to the amount of emotion that groups or individuals can tolerate.

Point C represents high intensity and emotional involvement, the inability to receive new information, understand other perspectives, or voice clearly one's concerns.

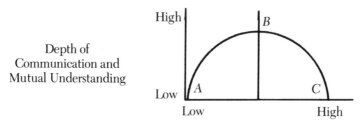

4. TWO OLD WAYS TO PLAY THE GAME OR A NEW WAY

Roger Fisher and William Ury in *Getting to Yes* ask what game one should play in a conflict: To be nice or to be tough? To yield to pressure or to apply pressure?

They propose a third way, which is neither soft nor hard but offers new options and fresh hope for resolution. It is called a *principled* way.

PROBLEM: WHICH GAME SHOULD YOU PLAY?		SOLUTION: CHANGE THE GAME!
SOFT	HARD	PRINCIPLED
Participants are friends.	Participants are adversaries.	Participants are problem-solvers.
The goal is agreement.	The goal is victory.	The goal is a wise outcome reached efficiently and amicably.
Make concessions to cultivate the relationship.	Demand concessions as a condition of the relationship.	Separate the people from the problem.
Be soft on the people and the problem.	Be hard on the problem and the people.	Be soft on the people, hard on the problem.
Trust others.	Distrust others.	Proceed independently of trust.
Change your positions easily.	Dig in to your position.	Focus on interests, not positions.
Make offers.	Make threats.	Explore interests..
Disclose your bottom line.	Mislead as to your bottom line.	Avoid having a bottom line.
Accept one-sided losses to reach settlement.	Demand one-sided gains as the price of agreement.	Invent options for mutual gain.
Search for the single answer: the one your opponent will accept.	Search for the single answer: the one you will accept.	Develop multiple options to choose from; decide later.

Insist on agree-ment.	Insist on your position.	Insist on using objective criteria.
Try to avoid a contest of will.	Try to win a contest of will.	Try to reach a result based on standards inde-pendent of will.
Yield to pressure.	Apply pressure	Reason and be open to reasoning; yield to principle, not pressure.

From *Getting to Yes,* by Roger Fisher and William Ury. Copyright © 1981 by Roger Fisher and William Ury. Reprinted by permission of Houghton Mifflin Company.

5. FIVE STYLES OF CONFLICT MANAGEMENT

Ron Kraybill offers a model for conflict management similar to ones used by Thomas-Kilmann and others. Compare also the diagram by David Augsburger ("Moving from Lose-Lose to Win-Win"). In Kraybill's model the roles are represented by images of a shark, an owl, a fox, a turtle, and a teddy bear.

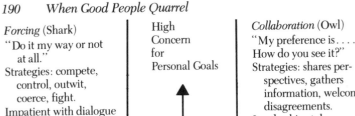

High
Concern
for
Personal Goals

Forcing (Shark)
"Do it my way or not
  at all."
Strategies: compete,
control, outwit,
coerce, fight.
Impatient with dialogue
Leadership style:
•authoritarian
•threatened by
  disagreement
•maintains status quo
•reacts to crisis
•pushes for quick fix

Collaboration (Owl)
"My preference is . . . .
How do you see it?"
Strategies: shares per-
spectives, gathers
information, welcomes
disagreements.
Leadership style:
•focuses on process
•open to change
•energized by
  differences
•prevents crisis by plan-
  ning
•quick to delegate

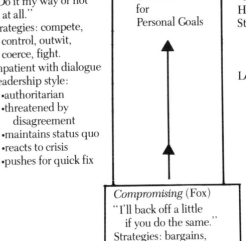

Compromising (Fox)
"I'll back off a little
  if you do the same."
Strategies: bargains,
reduces expectations,
something for everyone.
Tolerates exchange of
views but is
uncomfortable
Leadership style:
•cautious but open
•caring but controlling
•"Let's be reasonable"
•seeks lowest common
  denominator

Low Concern for
Relationship

High Concern for
Relationship

Avoiding (Turtle)

"Conflict? What
  conflict?"
Strategies: flee, withdraw.
ignore, delay.
Refuses to dialogue or
gather information

Leadership style:
•passive and timid
•"weathers the storm"
•inclined to
  spiritualize
•becomes unfocused

Low
Concern
for
Personal
Goals

Accommodating (Teddy
Bear)
"Whatever you say . . . ."
Strategies: agree, give in,
flatter, "being nice."
Interested in another's information and approval
Leadership style:
•ineffective in group
  settings
•easily swayed
•needs to please
  everyone
•threatened by people
  who don't talk

6. SIX STAGES OF MEDIATION

Writers on conflict resolution outline in a variety of ways the mediation process. Ron Kraybill outlines simple, helpful steps for the work of the third-party mediator.

(1) *Gaining Entry*

Present information about possible contributions of a third party.

(2) *Introduction*

Affirm parties' willingness to work face-to-face.

Describe procedure:(a) each gives own perspectlve, (b) identify key issues, (c) discuss issues one at a time.

Clarify that mediator guides discussion process, does not judge.

Gain commitment to ground rule: no interrupting of others.

(3) *Storytelling*

Each party explains situation from own perspective (starting with complainant) followed by mediator summary.

Confirm hearing. Each party summarizes the other's perspective to the other's satisfaction.

(4) *Problem-Solving*

Define issues, listing on wall chart.

Begin with easiest issue; continue one at a time.

   Ground rule: ideas first, evaluation second.

   (a) List ideas.

   (b) Evaluate: "My preference is . . . because . . ." or list impact of each idea on each party.

   (c) Decide/negotiate:

      Highlight commonalities.

      Ask parties to state what they need from each other.

      Paraphrase feelings and/or coach direct dialogue.

      Caucus when stalled.

(5) *Agreement*

Be specific: who, what, when, where.

Mediator summarizes agreement to both parties.

Anticipate how future difficulties shall be handled.

Commit agreement to paper and sign, giving copies to both.

(6) *Thanksgiving*

Thank the parties.

Give opportunity to state commitments to live up to agreement and
to renew cooperation.

Thank the Lord.

FOR FURTHER STUDY

LITERATURE

"A Guide to Peace Resources." Two-page guide with one hundred entries on such topics as "Biblical Studies," "Periodicals," "Peace Organizations," "Study Guides." Available free of charge from Mennonite Central Committee, Akron, Pa.

Augsburger, David. *Caring Enough to Confront.* Scottdale, Pa.: Herald Press, 1980. Description of a lifestyle for Christians who care enough to risk confronting others when differences become important.

Beer, Jenny. *Peacemaking in Your Neighborhood: Reflections on an Experiment in Community Mediation.* Philadelphia: New Society Publishers, 1986. Describes an innovative program with ten years of dispute settlement experience in the Philadelphia area.

Buzzard, Lynn, and Eck, Laurence. *Tell It to the Church.* Elgin, Ill.: D. C. Cook, 1982; Wheaton, Ill.:Tyndale, 1985. Two leaders of the Christian Conciliation Service describe a biblical approach to resolving conflict out of court.

Curle, Adam. *Making Peace.* London: Tavistock Pubs., 1971. Recognizes role of injustice in conflict situations.

Doyle, Michael, and Straus, David. *How to Make Meetings Work.* Jove ed. New York: Berkeley Publishing Group, 1982. Practical skills for facilitating meetings and decision-making.

Filley, Alan C. *Interpersonal Conflict Resolution.* Glenview, Ill.: Scott, Foresman and Company, 1975. An analytical look at sources of conflict and methods of conflict resolution, problem-solving, and decision-making.

Fisher, Roger, and Ury, William. *Getting to Yes: Negotiating Agreement Without Giving In.* Boston: Houghton Mifflin Co., 1981. Contains practical counsel for negotiating agreements.

Frost, Joyce, and Wilmot, William. *Interpersonal Conflict.* Dubuque, Iowa: W. C. Brown Co., 1978. A systematic examination of the factors that contribute to conflict with a focus on the communicative behavior of the participants.

Jackson, Dave. *Dial 911.* Scottdale, Pa.: Herald Press, 1981. Stories of peaceful Christians responding to urban violence on Chicago's north side.

Kraybill, Ronald S. *Repairing the Breach: Ministering in Community Conflict.* Akron, Pa.: Mennonite Central Committee. A useful guide for persons interested in community and congregational conflict resolution. 95 pages.

Leas, Speed. *A Lay Person's Guide to Conflict Management*. Washington, D.C.: The Alban Institute, 1979. 15 pages.

Leas, Speed, and Kittlaus, Paul. *Church Fights: Managing Conflict in the Local Church*. Philadelphia: Westminster Press, 1973. Strategy for resolving congregational conflicts. 186 pages.

Mock, Ron, ed. *The Role Play Book*. Akron, Pa.: Mennonite Conciliation Service, 1988. Thirty-two hypothetical situations for the practice of interpersonal peacemaking skills.

Moore, Christopher. *The Mediation Process*. San Francisco: Jossey Bass, 1986. A current survey and analysis of the role of the mediator.

Peace and Change. Vol. 8, No. 2/3. Summer 1982. A special issue on conflict resolution with fourteen articles by well-known practitioners. Center for Peaceful Change, Kent State University, Kent, Ohio 44242.

Walton, Richard E. *Interpersonal Peacemaking: Confrontation and Third Party Consultation*. Reading, Mass.: Addison-Wesley Publishing Company, 1969.

When You Disagree. Akron, Pa.: Mennonite Conciliation Service, 1987. A cassette tape learning package of ten units on topics ranging from developing personal styles in conflict to decision-making in congregations.

Zehr, Howard. *Mediating the Victim/Offender Conflict*. Mennonite Central Committee, 1980. Explores use of mediation as an alternative in criminal justice.

ORGANIZATIONS

Alban Institute. 4125 Nebraska Ave. N.W., Washington, D.C. 20016. Books, pamphlets, and seminars on dispute resolution in religious settings.

American Bar Association Committee on Dispute Resolution. 1800 M St. N.W., Suite 200, Washington, D.C. 20036. Information clearinghouse and free quarterly newsletter.

Community Boards Program, Inc., 149 Ninth St., San Francisco, CA 94103. Training in mediation skills for disputes in schools, workplaces, neighborhoods, and cross-cultural conflicts. Offers written and video training materials. Frequently schedules three- and four-day training institutes.

CDR Associates/Center for Dispute Resolution, 100 Arapahoe Ave., Boulder, CO 80302. Provides trained intervenors for conflicts involving family, schools, public policy issues, and business. Available to do mediation trainings.

Interfaith Conciliation Center, 404 S. 19th St., La Crosse, WI 54601. Promotes mediation skills in the church community. A clearinghouse of information about church-based resources and trainings.

Mennonite Conciliation Service. Box M, Akron, PA 17501. Network of mediators and workshop leaders on dispute resolution. Quarterly newsletter on techniques, resources, and training opportunities. Bibliographies and audio-visual materials available.

National Association of Mediation in Education, C/o Mediation Project, 425 Amity St., Amherst, MA 01002. Newsletter, workshops, and resources for teaching conflict resolution skills to students at all levels.

National Conference on Peacemaking and Conflict Resolution, C/o Center for Conflict Resolution, George Mason University, 4400 University Dr., Fairfax, VA 22030. Convenes peacemakers' conferences every eighteen months.

VORP/PACT, Institute of Justice, 901 Washington St., POB 177, Michigan City, IN 46360. Victim-Offender Reconciliation program. Publishes a newsletter. Serves as a clearinghouse for VORP programs nationwide.

SCRIPTURE INDEX

THE AUTHORS

Robert S. Kreider is a historian (Ph.D., University of Chicago) who has taught history and peace studies on the faculties of Bluffton (Ohio) College and Bethel College, North Newton, Kansas. He has served as an academic dean and college president. Kreider has frequently traveled abroad on assignments for the Mennonite Central Commitee, Mennonite World Conference, and China Educational Exchange. Recently he retired as Professor of Peace Studies and Director of the Kansas Institute for Peace and Conflict Resolution. With Rachel Waltner Goossen he wrote *Hungry, Thirsty, a Stranger: The MCC Experience* (Herald Press, 1988). Kreider and his wife, Lois, live in North Newton, Kansas, and are members of Faith Mennonite Church. They are the parents of five children.

Rachel Waltner Goossen is a doctoral student in American history at the University of Kansas. A native of Newton, Kansas, she graduated from Bethel College and received an M.A. from the University of California, Santa Barbara. Goossen served a one-year internship with the Mennonite Library and Archives and subsequently taught courses in public history at Bethel College. With Robert Kreider she coauthored *Hungry, Thirsty, a Stranger.* She is the author of two congregational histories, *Prairie Vision: The Pleasant Valley Mennonite Church* (1988) and *Meetingplace: A History of the Mennonite Church of Normal* (1987). Goossen and her husband, Duane, live in Goessel, Kansas. She is a member of Goessel Mennonite Church.